FROM PHYSICS TO METAPHYSICS

FROM PHYSICS TO METAPHYSICS

Francis Selman

The Saint Austin Press
296, Brockley Road, London, SE4 2RA
MMI

THE SAINT AUSTIN PRESS
296, Brockley Road
London, SE4 2RA

Telephone: +44 (0)20 8692 6009
Facsimile: +44 (0)20 8649 3609

Electronic Mail: books@saintaustin.org
http://www.saintaustin.org

ISBN 1 901157 33 4

Dedication

Máire Hickey, O.S.B.

Typeset and printed by NEWTON Design & Print, London, UK
http://www.newtondp.co.uk

CONTENTS

PREFACE

We live in an age when an enormous amount of information is readily available but there is little noticeable wisdom. Wisdom takes an overall view of life, concerns itself with the lasting purpose of human life and seeks a unified view of the world. We have rather lost the view of philosophy as the love of wisdom. As the streams of philosophy that have been dominant for the past century show signs of running into the sand, some writers are saying that we need to return to the earlier tradition of philosophy to show us the way forward.

At the same time Pope John Paul II in his recent encyclical, *Faith and Reason*, which perhaps more than any of his other writings caught the interest of the general public and the scholarly world, irrespective of religious belief, has underlined the value of philosophy and especially called for a return to metaphysics. Of the four main branches of philosophy (logic, epistemology, metaphysics and ethics), metaphysics may be regarded as the central one, for logic provides the rules of valid reasoning but does not tell us whether anything exists. While what we think exists partly depends on what we can know, equally we cannot know anything unless it first exists. Thus epistemology comes into metaphysics, but metaphysics provides the foundation of knowledge and of truth, which is the end of all our knowing.

The conclusion of this book indicates the relevance of metaphysics for the practical life and ethics. This book is designed to show how metaphysics enters into questions about the world around us and is required by the natural science that has especially influenced our way of thinking in the West for over a century.

I would like to thank Mr Ashley Paver at The Saint Austin Press for all his patient work in preparing the text for publication. I am especially grateful to Prof. Peter Geach not only for kindly supplying the Foreword of this book but also for reading the entire manuscript and pointing out a number of inaccuracies. The remaining errors are my own.

F.J. Selman.

September, 2000.

FOREWORD

Philosophy, as has been well said, starts with wonder: wonder at the way things are. Children's questions often have deep philosophical meaning... Gareth Matthews has published two volumes illustrating this, and Lewis Carroll's *Alice* books recapture our childish wonderment. These books have been translated into many languages, and even transcend cultural divisions; there is an adapted version of *Alice in Wonderland* in an Australian Aboriginee language. Such musings have a universal human appeal, especially in childhood; the practical needs and varied distractions of adult life usually make people forget these childish things, but not always; I once heard two working-men in a Leeds pub arguing keenly about whether it is right to say "Tomorrow never comes".

Philosophical enquiry is distinguished from these first beginnings by its persistence, generality, and rigour. *Persistence* means: going on developing thoughts till they at least seem to give a clear picture. Philosophic thought is *general*; it takes in the whole world and asks whether there is something beyond all present experience. The ideal of *rigour* is itself something that philosophizing at least teaches us to aim at, however often and however gravely philosophers have fallen short of that ideal. Rigour transformed geometry from hand-surveyors' rules to techniques for reasoning out what may be inferred from data about the dimensions of things.

Father Selman's book summarizes the long history of this systematic enquiry, from its beginnings in Ionian Greeks' speculations about the make-up and large-scale processes of the world. Philosophy has uninterruptedly grown from this like a tree from a seed. People often complain that philosophy "never gets anywhere". In fact, such sciences as physics, chemistry and biology were originally parts of the general enquiry and speculation.. What is more, a great number of our most familiar words and concepts can be traced back to philosophical discussions of past centuries. We would be very badly off without "quantity", "quality", and "relation"; these words come from the search for Latin equivalents of Aristotle's technicalities. Similarly for language we use to label features of language: "noun", "verb", "sentence", represent concepts shaped first in Plato's dialogues. Even when we do not intend to engage in philosophy, our very language is permeated with the results of past philosophers' hard thinking.

To pursue the metaphor of the tree, some branches that have grown have been useless or harmful; but there is a main line of healthy development. It appears to me that Father Selman observes a due balance in his history; his main effort is to get people to contribute to the healthy growth, or at least appreciate it.

Much main-line philosophy has consisted of speculation about the superhuman and supernatural: about a being or beings who control the processes of the world, about their attitude to humankind and about what attitude mankind should have towards them. From this there developed classical natural philosophy; here there was long a place for shared discussion between Christians, Jews and Muslims. A man may think these are not suitable topics for reasoned discussion; but then he had better only *preach*, not *argue* in favour of this attitude, or he contradicts himself. Awe before a deity precisely *for* being above all reason and logic is like admiring a tyrant for his uncontrolled caprices; indeed, the one may lead on to the other; men have been led on from irrationalist theology to adulation of leaders "above" ordinary decencies. Logic is named from *logos*, and "Logos" is the name of the Divine Reason by which the world was made.

Human beings, made to reflect that Reason in their small measure, may hope to progress in understanding the world; history shows this hope not to have been vain. "All mind is alike", said Anaxagoras, "the greater and the lesser."

P.T. Geach.

Chapter One

WHAT IS METAPHYSICS?

It is not easy to say what metaphysics is without using a word
that seems to tell us little or no more. It will be by studying the
various aspects of what this other word names that we shall
come to understand what metaphysics is. We may start, then,
by saying that metaphysics is about reality or what really exists.
By reality, I mean the sum of everything in the world outside
us, in the sense that anyone who thinks the world is unreal
thinks that it is just an idea in his mind. Thinkers, however,
have disagreed about what sorts of things really exist. Some
have said that the only things that exist are material, others
that there are also immaterial ones. The most widespread view
at present is that the only things which really exist are things
that natural science studies: things we can perceive with the
senses, see, hear, touch and measure with instruments. This is
the *empiricist* view, that unless something can be studied by
science or verified by the senses, it does not really exist. This
view leaves no room for metaphysics, since it says that there is

nothing beyond what can be known by scientific inquiry; physics is sufficient without any need for metaphysics.

Metaphysics is the title of one of the main works of Aristotle. It was not given this title by Aristotle himself, but comes from the time when his works were collected at the library of Alexandria in the third century B.C. — either because this work came next after his *Physics* in the collection, or because it is about things which lie beyond the realm of physics and natural science. The only times that Aristotle calls his metaphysics anything, it is either "first philosophy" or "theology".[1] "Meta" means "after" and "beyond".

Perhaps the easiest way to understand what metaphysics means is to leave out the prefix "meta" to begin with, and just consider physics, with which we are more familiar. The word "physics" comes from *phusis*, the Greek word for nature. Physics, then, was the ancient equivalent for natural science. Although we take the word "nature" for granted, the concept of nature first had to be worked out. This was the achievement of Aristotle, who defined nature as everything with its own principle of movement and rest.[2] Movement for Aristotle primarily meant the change from one state to another, rather than motion from place to place. Natural things have a principle of change in themselves: acorns turn into oak trees and carbon crystallizes into diamonds by natural action, but copper does not turn into a kettle or clay into a pot by itself.

So Aristotle said that everything is either made "by nature or by art". A sheep produces wool by nature but a glove does not come from wool by nature; it is made by the art of knitting. The Greek word for art is *techne*, from which we get our word "technology"; we use technology for making

---

[1] *Metaphysics* IV c.1; VI c.1.
[2] *Physics* II c.1 192b12.

things like radios and telephones and everything we make with our knowledge of natural science. Things made by art come from a mind, for an artist or craftsman first has to have an idea of what he is going to make. But nature produces things automatically: a peacock automatically puts forth a new fan tail every spring.

But what about nature itself? Has it come about by chance or has it, too, been produced by someone with an idea of what he was making? It is clear from the design of the parts and organs of plants and animals that many things in nature have a purpose or function. But in order to move or act with an aim, one needs to have a conception of what one is aiming at. Neither the sea nor stones have a conception of what they are doing as they move. When natural things regularly act for a purpose or end without having a conception of what they are doing, we may suppose that nature has been made by someone who has given everything its way of acting according to its nature. Thomas Hobbes (1588-1679) called nature "the art of God".[3]

THEORETICAL SCIENCE

We next look at the relation of physics to other sciences. Science for Aristotle is about the principles (*archai*) of things. Theoretical, or speculative, sciences pursue the truth about things for its own sake. Aristotle divides the theoretical sciences into three: physics, mathematics and divine science. By physics, he means natural science. Natural science studies things which move: particles and photons, liquids and light waves. We want to know whether they move purely at random or for a reason; in other words, we want to know why things

---

[3] *Leviathan*, Introduction, first sentence. Cf. Plato, *Sophist* 265c.

happen and what their cause is. If things do not just move at random in any unpredictable way but for a reason, because they have a cause, the universe is a *rational* one and has been made by an Intelligence. The pursuit of science presupposes that the universe is rational, otherwise it would not be possible to discover why things act as they do in nature, but only to record a series of events without any apparent connection. "In the beginning was the Logos."[4] *Logos* means both "word" and "reason".

Mathematics is about things which do not move or change in themselves: the properties of numbers and geometrical figures cannot be altered. Although geometrical shapes are found in bodies that move, mathematics considers them on their own apart from material bodies: for example, it considers a sphere apart from the matter of a solid sphere. Where physics is about the laws of nature, mathematics is about the laws of the laws of nature, for the laws of nature are expressed in the terms of mathematics or algebra. Mathematics is itself *logical*, so a universe in which we can discover laws of nature that can be expressed in mathematical terms is a rational one.

Divine science is the science of God or *theology*. As physics is about moving things and mathematics about unchanging things, though found in moving things, so there is a third science about something which is altogether unmovable. We may suppose that there is such a science, because physics is about the causes of moving things, but we do not come to an end of asking about causes until we come back to the first cause of all. The first cause, however, cannot itself be moved, or else there would be a question about what moves its mover, and so on. So there is something immovable

---

[4] St. John, 1:1.

preceding all moving things, and we have to go *beyond* physics, which is about moving things, in order to come to the cause of all the causes that physics studies. When we study the natural world, as we do in physics, we ask about causes and this leads us back to the first cause. Aristotle calls divine science or theology "the most noble, because God is thought to be the cause of all things".[5]

Physics tells us *how* things act but it does not tell us *why* they exist. Metaphysics is about the most general causes of things existing; and so it is about what makes anything be.

NATURAL QUESTIONS

We also quite quickly come to metaphysics by considering some examples from everyday life. Let us take an ordinary sentence like "Copenhagen was a horse." (Copenhagen was the Duke of Wellington's horse.) This apparently simple sentence straightaway raises several questions. First, what made Copenhagen a horse? Presumably, it was something that he shared in common with other horses. But this was not the matter of his body, because he was a separate unit of flesh and bones from every other horse; so it was something else that he had in common with other horses — a certain *form*. If all horses have the same form, our next question is whether there is just one form of a horse, in which all horses share, as Plato thought. But horses are not all related to some form that exists outside them, for each horse has its own form. A horse is not just its form, because it is by nature also a body. Am I, for instance, just my form? Not if I am a corporeal being. So matter as well as form is part of the nature, or essence, of a horse and a human being. What makes horses different one

---

[5] *Metaphysics* I c.2 983a5.

from another is that each is an individual lump of matter; what makes them the same kind of thing is their form. Their form makes them be horses rather than giraffes or zebras.

Let us now take another horse, called Pegasus. Unlike Copenhagen, Pegasus was not a real horse. He was the winged horse ridden by Bellerophon of Greek mythology; but he never existed. This gives us the difference between things that have existed in reality and things that have existed only in men's minds, like the characters of fiction. But how can we sensibly ask what Pegasus is when he has not existed, for it seems that he is nothing if he did not exist? Yet we are able to say what Pegasus is: a winged horse. So how can we say what he is unless he existed in some way after all, and there *is* something that he is? Thus the example of Pegasus quickly leads us to questions about *existence*.[6]

For my third example, I shall take a hyacinth bulb. We would normally say that a bulb is not a plant and a plant is not a bulb; therefore they are two different kinds of thing. But one and the same thing was once a bulb and is now a hyacinth, for they have a continuous existence. When a hyacinth comes from a bulb, is this just an alteration of the bulb or has something new come into existence, for a hyacinth now exists in the room where previously there was no hyacinth? Are bulbs and hyacinths just modifications of one great mass of matter or can we talk about individual things coming into and going out of existence?

By asking quite natural questions about ordinary things like horses and hyacinths, we have come across some of the main topics of metaphysics: matter and form, nature or essence, cause and existence. Metaphysics is not just about abstract things; rather it is thinking abstractly about ordinary

---

[6] The idea of Pegasus comes from W.V.O. Quine, "On What There Is", in *A Logical Point of View* (Harvard, 1953), pp.1-19.

things in the world around us. We do not just ask about the material properties and qualities of the things that we perceive with the senses, but also whether things just consist of their material properties and sensible qualities, and what it is for them to exist at all.

Physics and chemistry study the material properties of things, but do not ask whether they are just their material properties. For this question, we have to go beyond physics to metaphysics. Aristotle called metaphysics "first philosophy", because it is about what all the things studied by the other sciences have in common, which is quite simply that they *exist*. Thus metaphysics is said to be about "being" or, as I think it is better to say, about *existent* things: *ta onta*, in Aristotle's phrase, "the things that are".

Aristotle describes three stages in the development of Western philosophy. At first, philosophers only thought about things as they are this and that thing; then they thought about them as they are kinds of thing; finally, they came to consider them simply as they exist. These three stages correspond to the early physicists, Plato and Aristotle respectively. To begin with, philosophers asked about the material constituents of things, then about form, and finally about the two together as things are substances. These three stages provide the topics of the next three chapters. If metaphysics may be said to begin with Plato, we should remember that in part he developed his philosophy as an answer to questions he had inherited from his predecessors. To understand Plato, then, we first need to take a look at the background of his thought in the Presocratic philosophers. They, too, will show us how from physics we come to metaphysics.

Chapter Two

MATTER AND MOTION

The first philosophers in the West were called "physicists" (*phusikoi*) by Aristotle, because they inquired about nature. They wanted to know the cause of the great variety of forms of things in the natural world and what was the source of motion and change. They were the natural scientists of their time, and science began with philosophers wanting to know what the world is made of. Newton (1642-1727) was not known as a "scientist" but as a "natural philosopher", and it was still quite common to call scientists "natural philosophers" into the nineteenth century. Dr. Johnson, writing in the eighteenth century, records in his *Journey to the Western Isles* that one day he found nothing of "philosophic interest" in the terrain he crossed, by which he meant nothing of interest for the botanist or geologist. Aristotle says that the beginning of philosophy is a sense of wonder.[1] The earliest philosophers

---

[1] *Metaphysics* I c.2.

were filled with wonder as they observed the phenomena of nature.

They were especially struck by one thing in nature – change – and sought to explain its cause. To ask about the cause of change is to ask about motion, for things change by moving. Physics is the study of motion. Their question was: what is the principle (*arche*) of change? As one thing comes from another in nature, one may suppose that all change goes back to one cause. Some of the first philosophers thought that the principle of nature was one, others that it was many. Most of those who thought that it was one thought that it was movable, but Parmenides thought it was immovable. At first, they looked for the principle of the world in its material constituents. The ancients believed that the sub-lunar world was made of four elements (*stoicheia*), which they said were air, fire, water and earth. They could not know that the stars are also made of the same chemical elements as the earth, but seeing that they are apparently immovable, unlike things beneath the moon, they thought they consisted of a fifth element, from which we get our word "quintessence".

The ancient theory of the four elements is not as unscientific as it appears to be, for these elements correspond to the different states of matter in modern chemistry. Air stands for gas, water for liquids and earth for solids. If we were to suggest an equivalent for fire, it would be radiation, since twentieth century physics has shown us that matter can be converted into radiation. The difference between the ancient and modern theories of the elements is that a chemical element today, by definition, does not consist of other elements but, in the ancient theory, one element could change into another. Water, for example, can be converted into vapour by being heated and into a solid state by being cooled.

Solids too can be converted into liquids by being melted, as with molten metal.

Thus some of the early philosophers took one of the elements, air or water or fire, to be the principle of everything else. None of them suggested that it was earth, for solid matter by itself is inert, unless moved by something else; but the wind (air) and sea (water) are in perpetual motion. Those who derived everything from a single material principle regarded the world as one great substance and everything in it as modifications of a single mass of matter.

THE IONIANS

The first philosopher known to us is Thales (c. 625-545 B.C.). He was the only one of the Seven Wise Men of ancient Greece who asked about the causes of nature. He thought that the primary element was water. His successor was Anaximander (c.610-540 B.C.), whose pupil was Anaximenes (c.600-530 B.C.). Anaximenes and Diogenes thought that air was the first principle. Men thought that water or air was the primary element, because one way to explain motion in the world is to liken the world to a living body, for living things move themselves, and all living things need air and water to live.

Anaximander, however, noticed that the elements come in pairs of contraries: water and fire, which are wet and dry; air and earth, which are light and heavy. Therefore, he thought that the principle of the world could not be one but must be many. He said that the world comes from matter being indeterminate and in continual motion. Heraclitus (c. 500 B.C.) also held that matter is in continual motion, but took fire to be the primary element, for this is the most volatile and movable, as well as the most subtle, of the elements.

Thus we get the following list of the four elements, with their chief proponents:

Ancient Element	Modern State	Philosopher
Fire	Radiation	Heraclitus
Air	Gas	Anaximenes
Water	Liquid	Thales
Earth	Solid	

Anaximander saw that an element can pass from one state to another either by becoming rarer or more dense. Thus moisture turns into air as it is spread out, air turns into liquid when it condenses, and a liquid may solidify when it is compressed.

All these philosophers so far looked for a material cause of the world. The first to say that it also had an *efficient* cause was Anaxagoras (c. 500-428 B.C.). He was also the first to say that the world was made by a mind. The mind for him was a moving force. Like Anaximander, he thought that the world was made of infinitely many kinds of matter, which he said were all mixed up to begin with in an indistinct mass and were drawn out by Mind (*Nous*) into distinct kinds of thing. He saw that Mind could not be mixed like material elements. Otherwise, it would be one of them and unable to draw them out. Therefore, it must be unmixed and immaterial. Although Anaxagoras held that the world was made by Mind, we should note that he does not explain how matter came to be there in the first place, but presupposes that it already existed in a confused mass.

Contemporary with Anaxagoras was Empedocles (c.495-433 B.C.), who was not an Ionian but lived in Acragas in Sicily. Empedocles, seeing that the four elements were insufficient to explain motion, added two separate causes of motion: love and strife. Thus, he was the first to introduce the idea of forces operating on matter. His love and strife correspond with attraction and repulsion. In the scheme of Empedocles, love combines the elements to form bodies of various kinds aand then strife separates the elements to form heaps of the same element. There is rest when everything is blended by love; then strife stirs and motion begins again. But Empedocles does not explain why love and strife alternate in gaining the ascendency over one another. Nor are Empedocles' love and strife purely mechanical forces, for he seems to have conceived them on a moral pattern, as love brings people together and strife separates them. We may, however, see in Empedocles' cyclic process of the world the forerunner of the theory of the oscillating universe, held by some astronomers of the present time.

ATOMIC THEORY

Democritus (c. 460-370 B.C.) was the younger contemporary of Empedocles. Reflecting on Anaximander's theory that matter changes by expanding and contracting, Democritus saw that if the same quantity of matter can take up a greater or smaller space, it cannot be continuous but must consist of particles, which can separate. These he called "atoms", the smallest units of matter, which cannot be cut up any further. Democritus then had little difficulty in explaining motion, because when atoms move apart, they will move around in the empty space between them. In moving around at random, some will collide and build groups of atoms and eventually larger bodies. He thought that all the various kinds of matter and natural things come from the weaving together of atoms of certain basic shapes: hooked, angular, curved, sinuous and so on. Whereas Anaxagoras thought there was just one world, Democritus thought there were innumerable worlds, as he supposed that everything came about by the chance movement of particles of matter. The view that there are many worlds has become common again today.

PYTHAGORAS AND PARMENIDES

To go back a little in time before Democritus, at the same time as the Ionians lived around the eastern shore of the Aegean Sea, two philosophers of a quite different cast of mind arose to the west of Greece, in southern Italy. These were Pythagoras, the discoverer of the harmonic scale, and Parmenides. Pythagoras (c. 530 B.C.) was a mathematician and thought that the variety of natural things was not so much to be explained by different elements as by the proportion, or ratio, in which they are combined. He held that different sorts of matter are due to different *configurations* of elements, just as modern chemistry reveals that the atoms of molecules combine in regular geometrical figures, like cubes and hexagons. We can explain the difference between water and sulphuric acid, for example, by the different ratio of hydrogen to oxygen atoms. Water has two of hydrogen to one of oxygen (H_2O), sulphuric acid the same two of hydrogen but with four of oxygen and one of sulphur (H_2SO_4). This may help us to see why Pythagoras thought that things are composed of numbers and that the structure of the physical world is mathematical.

Pythagoras may not explain motion, but he provides the mathematical way of looking at the universe, which later enabled Galileo (1564-1642) to express general laws of nature in a mathematical way for the first time. Galileo said that nature "is written in mathematical language and its characters are geometrical figures". Some physicists today think that the world could be given a completely mathematical description. We may understand this when we recall that sculptors and architects begin a statue or a building by first drawing in lines the main proportions and basic geometrical shapes of the structures they intend to make.

Parmenides (c. 520-450 B.C.) had no need to explain change, because he simply denied that there was any change. He reasoned like this: either something is or it is not. If it is, it does not come to be, since it already is. If it is not, it also does not come to be, since nothing comes from what is not, that is from nothing. So either a thing is, or it cannot even come to be. Hence there is no becoming, but only being. For Parmenides, something either is altogether or not at all; there is no in between stage, as for instance in a caterpillar becoming a butterfly. Nor does Parmenides allow for things coming into existence, as icicles do in winter, since everything already simply is. There is only unchanging being for Parmenides, and all change is an illusion. But this plainly contradicts the evidence of our senses, for things clearly come into existence, which did not exist there before.

There is a direct tradition from Parmenides to Plato, since Socrates, who was the teacher of Plato, tells us that he once met Parmenides as a young man, when Parmenides was already advanced in age. The philosophy of Plato can be seen to come from a combination of Pythagoras and Parmenides. From Pythagoras, he drew the idea of form, as variety is explained by ratios and geometrical shapes; from Parmenides, he took up the idea of being. As it was not possible to sustain Parmenides' view of unchanging being in this changing world, Plato used Pythagoras' idea of form to solve the difficulty by putting unchanging being in another world — that of the Forms.

Our brief account of the Presocratics may have served to show that the same philosophy of the early physicists, which gave birth to natural science, also led to metaphysics. By only looking for material principles of the world, they failed to progress, because they did not attend to the complementary idea of *form*.

Chapter Three

FORM

Form is a rather neglected topic in modern philosophy. But everything has a form: a glass, a piece of furniture, a flower has a distinct form. Metals and minerals have different forms as they have different structures: basalt differs from granite and jade by its form. Animals too differ by their forms; what distinguishes a lion from an antelope is that it has a different form, and what makes things belong to the same class, for example the lion class, is that they have the same form. From seeing that some things all share the same form, one may then go on to say that there is one form that they all share. This brings us to Plato's theory of Forms, that things are lions because they all share in the Lion Form, which exists on its own apart from all lions, and likewise for every kind of natural thing. Plato (427-347 B.C.) also called these forms "ideas", from the Greek word for shape or form *eidos* (plural *eidea*). Since the Forms or Ideas exist separately from visible things, he thought of them as immaterial objects. In this chapter, I propose first to say why Plato came to devise his theory of

Forms, then to examine the relation of the Forms to things in this world and the truth in his theory, before ending with some criticisms of the theory.

CERTAIN KNOWLEDGE

Plato's philosophy can be seen as a reaction to Heraclitus' claim that we cannot have certain knowledge of anything, for everything is in a continual state of flux and changing all the time. This is summed up in his dictum that you cannot step into the same river twice, because the second time a different mass of water is flowing past the same point. When something changes from moment to moment, it is not possible to check that it is as you say it is, for by the time you have said one thing about it, it is already different. One has only to think of a sunset, as the colours of the clouds shift quite rapidly. We find something similar to Heraclitus' view in modern physics with the Uncertainty Principle, which says that it is not possible to know the exact position and exact velocity of a particle simultaneously — only one or the other can be precisely known at any one time. If it is not possible to have certain knowledge of things in this changing material world, the alternative is to look for certain knowledge in a world of unchanging, immaterial objects. Thus Socrates, on hearing of Heraclitus' view, turned to abstract objects like the virtues for surer knowledge, and began asking, "What is courage? What is justice? What is knowledge itself?" To ask questions of this sort is to ask about the nature of justice, happiness, and so on. Thus the objects of proper knowledge for Socrates and Plato became the essences of things. Plato's Ideas are the essences of things. As certainty about changing things was thought to be impossible, in order to save the possibility of certain knowledge, Plato invented another world of unchanging objects, the Forms or Ideas.

Proper knowledge for Plato is of what *is*; if it is not, we cannot know it. So, knowledge is only of being. But changing things also share in non-being, for when they change they become something they were not, and cease to be something they were. As only what has being is real, Plato held that changing things are not altogether real, for they share in non-being as well as being. Only unchanging things can be the real things, because only they have being and no non-being in them. What does not change is not visible things but the ideas of them. For example, countless dolphins have come into and gone out of existence since Plato's time, but we may suppose that our idea of a dolphin is much the same as it was for the ancient Greeks twenty-four centuries ago. In other words, the idea of a dolphin, unlike the many dolphins, does not change and remains *constant*.

Plato's theory, then, arose from seeking a world of constant truth. Mathematics provides us with a science of constant truth. Natural scientists, too, say that there are certain "constants" in nature, like the speed of light.

Plato tells us a second reason why he devised his theory of Forms: because he was not just interested in beautiful things, but in knowing what beauty is itself.[1] Beauty itself is like the essence of beauty, considered on its own apart from beautiful things, yet shared in by everything beautiful. To think about beauty apart from beautiful things is to think of it abstractly. Therefore, the idea of beauty is not material like beautiful things. So Plato's Forms or Ideas are the essences of things: the Horse Form, for example, is the essence of a horse, or the essential horse, by sharing in which other things are

---

[1] Phaedo 100d.

horses. It seems reasonable to think that things are beautiful because they share, or *participate*, in beauty and, indeed, that they are beautiful because they have the Form of Beauty, just as things are horses because they share in the Horse Form. But Plato makes the Ideas or Forms exist on their own, because beautiful things are not identical with beauty itself.

Since things are beautiful because they share in beauty, beauty is the cause of things being beautiful. Thus Plato's Forms are the causes of things being what they are: the cause of something being a lion is that it shares in the Lion Form, according to Plato. But as beautiful things are not beauty itself, and lions are not *the* Lion itself, things are beautiful or lions because they *resemble* the Idea of Beauty or the Lion Idea. Thus Plato regarded things in this world as copies and imitations of the real things, which he thought were the Ideas existing in another, invisible world. The Forms or Ideas, therefore, are like the master copies and exemplars of things in this world, which are whatever they are because they share in the Forms. Likewise, the idea in the artist's mind is a cause of the picture he paints; it is also the exemplar of his painting. Thus Plato's philosophy is the source of a long tradition of seeing visible things as images of invisible realities.

We remember that the invisible Ideas were the real things for Plato, because the fact that they are unchanging means that only they have being. We may ask ourselves whether works of art are images of ideas or of real things that they depict. If a picture is painted according to the exemplar in the mind of the artist, but the artist's idea comes from something in the physical world, the picture is an image of the physical thing, not just of an idea.

Knowledge for Plato is of the Forms or Ideas, for these are the real things for him. What we have of changing things in this world, he says, is opinion rather than knowledge.[2] Things in this world are only copies and reflections of the real things, which exist on their own in another world removed from our senses. As the Forms are immaterial, it follows that they exist separately from the material things of which they are the form. When we think of abstract things like the virtues, it seems reasonable to suppose there is an invisible world of ideas, for justice itself is not anything visible, yet we would say that justice exists. Unless it exists, nothing can become just, and we would not be able to tell whether something had become just without something just by which to measure it. By starting out from immaterial things like virtues, Plato then applied his theory to the forms of material things, like lions and horses, as well.

TWO WORLDS

Plato draws a distinction between two worlds: an invisible world of unchanging Ideas, and the visible world of changing things. It is knowledge of the world of Ideas that gives us truth, for this is the real world; what we have of the visible world is sense perception, which does not count as real knowledge for Plato. His division of the two worlds may be represented by the diagram below.

World of Ideas	intelligible	knowledge	of truth	with the mind
World of Sensible Objects	visible	perception	of light	with the senses

The world of Ideas is a higher world, because it lies beyond the reach of the senses; only the mind can apprehend

---

[2] Republic VI 509e.

the Ideas. Plato says that we behold the Ideas with "the eye of the mind";[3] perhaps he was the first to coin this phrase. It is also a higher world, because the Forms are the causes of things in this world, which in their turn are mere copies and reflections of the real things in the world of Ideas.

It is interesting to note that a philosopher so different from Plato as David Hume drew a similar distinction between two worlds, this world and a world of ideas. He notes that in the world around us we find a sun, moon, mountains, rivers, houses and ships. When we come to the universe of ideas we find another set of similar objects: a sun, moon, mountains, ships and so on.[4] The difference between Plato and Hume is that, for Plato, this world mirrors the world of Ideas, whereas for Hume, the universe of ideas mirrors the world we perceive. For Plato, things in this world are images of the Ideas, which are the real things; for Hume, we have images in our mind of things in this world. Another difference is that Hume's universe of ideas is internal, in our minds, but Plato's world of Ideas is external, existing on its own.

TYPES AND TOKENS

The relation between things in this world and the Ideas, as Plato sees it, can be illustrated with an analogy from printing. In the days when compositors set type by hand, every printer had fonts of different typefaces. Even today, computers have fonts of various typefaces. A font contains so many pieces of each letter, numeral and punctuation mark. All the individual pieces are called tokens; what they are tokens of is one or another type. Each different letter and numeral is a type. So all

---

[3] Republic VI 510e.
[4] A Treatise of Human Nature, I iv 5.

the individual "a"s in the font are tokens of the type "lower-case 'a'"; all the "A"s are similarly tokens of the type "upper-case 'A'", and so on. All the tokens of each type were cut, or reproduced, from one master copy or exemplar. Thus the master copies of a printer's font are like Plato's Forms, and the tokens are like the things in this world, which Plato thought were copies of the Forms. For example, all swans are so many instances, or tokens, of the Swan Form.

When Plato says that the Forms are the real things, it is as though, in counting the number of bits of type in a font, we include the number of types as well as of tokens; or in stating the number of ducks on a pond we added the number of different varieties of duck to the number of individual birds swimming on the pond. But when we count ducks on a pond, we do not count some realities over and above the real ducks on the pond. There just are so many real ducks on the pond, which are instances of various types of duck. The mallard form, for example, is not a reality existing apart from the mallards we can see.

We discern in Plato's theory of the Forms a tendency to think that what makes two things alike is some *third* thing. Socrates once takes the example of two sticks and asks how we could see that one falls short of the other in length unless we already had the idea of equality, for we see that they are not equal like equality itself[5]. As two sticks of equal length or two straight lines sometimes appear to us equal, and sometimes unequal, though they remain the same all the time, the equality we know does not exist in the world of sense. Plato thought the idea of equality exists on its own in another world, and we know it as an innate idea — from having known it before this life, when the soul existed on its own and saw the Ideas.

---

[5] Phaedo 74a.

Plato's theory is that what makes two horses be horses is some third horse, which is the Horse of all horses, and what makes two beds be beds is a third bed, *the* Bed itself.

To see whether this is true, we may ask ourselves whether we see two or three things when we see two faces that are similar. Do I just see two faces or two faces and their similarity? The similarity does not exist on its own but lies in the two faces; we see two faces and judge them to be similar.

THE TRUTH IN PLATO

Plato's theory of the Ideas existing on their own as immaterial objects seems a good way of explaining how it is possible for many people to have the same idea of something, for example of a dolphin or swan. When many people share the same idea of a swan, there is *one* object of their thought; they do not have their own, subjective, ideas of a swan but an objective idea. We might think that many people would have their own, different ideas of a swan, unless there is some single thing in which they all participate. This thing will be an immaterial Idea, because material things vary, but the Idea is unvarying and the same.

Wittgenstein considers the thought that what names, such as "swan", "goldfinch" or "tree" signify must be indestructible; otherwise, if everything were destroyed it would not be possible to talk about them any more.[6] We can continue to do so, because we still have the ideas of what has been destroyed. So, even if all elm trees have been destroyed, the idea of the elm remains in existence. If names still signify, they must signify something. It seems, then, that what they signify has not been destroyed; but when the physical things

---

[6] Philosophical Investigations I 55, 57.

have been destroyed, this must be the idea. So, for example, if all red things were destroyed, the word "red" would not lose its meaning, and what it signified would seem to have an *independent* existence, just as Plato thought his Ideas existed independently of the things of which they were the ideas. But suppose that all red things were destroyed, would redness still exist? The idea of red would still exist, but not redness, unless the idea itself were red, which it is not. So redness would not exist after all, if all red things were destroyed, and we cannot say, with Plato, that the Idea of red is *the* real red thing.

Redness is a *universal*; it is what exists in all red things. The American logician, Quine, proposes that belief in the existence of universals arose from treating general words, such as "red", "square" and "human", like abstract singular words ("redness", "squareness" and "humanity"), and then thinking that squareness and humanity exist in themselves, as square things and human beings do.[7] But squareness does not exist on its own apart from square things like chess boards, any more than does whiteness, which is only found in white things. Colours and shapes only exist *in* things. A figure may be a square or a circle, but an idea cannot be; the idea of a circle is not itself round.

CRITICISM OF THE FORMS

Having considered what truth there is in Plato's theory of the Forms, we now set out some criticisms of it. Criticism of the Ideas was something which Plato began himself. For example, he raises the objection that, if the Forms are objects of thought and things participate in them, these things too will consist of thoughts. Then either everything will think, as it

---

[7] *From a Logical Point of View* (Harvard, 1953), pp.76f.

consists of thoughts, or there will be unthought thoughts.[8] But we know that things like armchairs do not think; so there are many things which do not consist of thoughts.

Another general problem of Plato's theory is that, if knowledge is of unchanging realities, how do we have proper knowledge of changing things in this world? A similar difficulty is raised by Plato: if the Forms are the objects of our knowledge, how can we know them, for they can only be known by Knowledge itself? As we do not possess knowledge itself, for it is a separate Idea, it seems that we cannot know the Ideas either.[9]

We will examine five further arguments against the theory of the Forms. First, Aristotle points out that if it is part of the nature of something to be corporeal, the Horse itself cannot be an immaterial Form or Idea. If being material is part of the Idea of something, the real sapphire cannot be an immaterial sapphire. The natures, or essences, of material things only *really* exist in matter, not as immaterial Ideas.

Second, if the real Horse is one thing, by sharing in which other things are horses, we face the following dilemma. The Horse Form either exists wholly or partly in a horse. If it exists wholly, it can only exist in one horse and many horses cannot share in the one Horse. Or, if it exists in many horses, it is divided between them and it ceases to be one thing in itself. But it seems that there can only be one Form of a horse, or else horses will not have the same Form and we will not be able to call them by the same name. If it exists wholly in anything, it cannot exist in many; if it exists partly in each one, something that is only partly a horse is not a horse, just as what is partly gold is not counted as real gold. Moreover, if a Form exists on its own, it cannot be the same in many things,

---

[8] Parmenides 132c.
[9] Ibid. 134b.

for they do not have the same existence, but each has its own existence.

We may explain Plato's theory like this: the real oyster is the oyster Idea, which we designate with a capital "O". All the oysters of flesh and shell that have lived in the sea are like little "o"s, which share in the big "O", as depicted below with the same division of the two worlds that we used above.

Real, intelligible world	Oyster Idea
Sensible, visible world	o o o o o o o oysters

Little "o"s are oysters that existed on this earth; they are oysters by virtue of sharing in big "O", the Oyster. As each little "o" has its own existence, big "O" cannot have the same existence in every little "o". Therefore, they do not have the same form by sharing in a separately existing Form and things are not oysters by sharing in the Oyster Form that exists on its own.

Third, Plato thought that the Forms were the essences of things: the Horse Form is the Horse itself, what makes all horses be horses. But what a thing is, which is its essence, cannot be anything existing separately from that thing. Socrates is not humanity, for he is not the only human being; but the humanity of Socrates, which makes him a human being, does not exist outside him on its own. I am not related to what I am, nor is my form external to me. What something is, is not another thing apart from the individual with that nature; the horse nature only really exists in individual horses of flesh and bone.

Fourth, Plato said that the Forms are the cause of the existence of things: what makes things beautiful is the form of beauty and what makes things be horses, is the Horse Form. Yet he supposed that the Forms were unchanging and so immobile. But as they are immobile, they cannot cause anything. Although the Forms are meant to cause the changing world, they do not explain change itself, for they cannot be the source of motion. Plato later saw that, if the forms could exist on their own as real objects, they would have to be able to *act*, for he once asked: "And must not Being have life and mind?"[10] In other words, the Ideas would only exist if they were minds and thought. As they are immaterial, their activity must likewise be immaterial. This is thinking.

Plato has many causes of the world as he has many Ideas, which exist on their own with no connection to one another, except that in one place he makes the primary cause of all existence the Idea of the Good, which he compares with the sun.[11] St. Augustine (d. 430), who was brought up on the doctrines of Plato, saw that the Ideas could be the causes and exemplars of things, if they were all put into the divine mind.[12] At the same time, this gives unity to all the Ideas, for they are the ideas of one mind, which is the cause of all things. Ideas are the causes of things, because no-one makes anything without first having an idea in his mind of what he intends to make: for example, the Louvre first existed as an idea in the mind of its architect.

Fifth, the theory that all horses are horses by virtue of another horse can be defeated by the following argument, known as the *Third Man Argument*. There is a man, the Form Man, by which all men are men. But as this Man is a man, he

---

[10] Sophist 248c.
[11] Republic VI 508e; VII 517c.
[12] Eighty-Three Questions, *Patrologia latina* vol.40 col.30, q.46,2.

and all men will be men by another man, a Third Man, which will also be a Form; and so on for ever. The argument that there is a man by which all men are men thus leads to a contradiction, for there is not one man but always another man by which they are men. Nor is there a horse through which all horses are horses, and Plato's theory that *the* Horse exists on its own apart from all horses is undermined. When we count ducks on the lake, there is not an additional reality, the Duck, besides them; the real ducks are just the ducks on the lake.

The question "Which are the real things?" lies at the heart of the difference between Plato and his pupil, Aristotle. For Plato, they are the unchanging Forms, because only they have being; when we see variable things in this world, it is as though we are looking at shadows of the real things, which exist in another world. But for Aristotle, the individual things we see in this world are the real things. For both, the real things are those from which they thought we get our ideas. Plato thought that this was from the Ideas themselves, which we know *innately*, because the soul sees them on their own before we are born into this world. But Aristotle held that we acquire our ideas from the things, which we perceive with our senses. Where the Presocratics looked for material causes of the world, and Plato made his Forms the causes of visible things, Aristotle was able to bring matter and form together in his doctrine of substance.

Chapter Four

SUBSTANCE

The word "substance" has undergone an almost complete reversal of its original meaning. Today, we use it of chemical substances: potassium, magnesium and tin are substances. We find this definition of chemistry in the Penguin Dictionary of Science: "the study of the composition of substances and their effects on one another". Chemical substances on their own, however, just exist in loose heaps without any definite shape. Silver is a substance in the modern sense of the word. But "substance" originally meant the individual things we make out of what are called substances today. In its original meaning, a silver spoon is a substance, because it is an individual thing, made out of silver. Silver is its matter, the spoon shape is its form. This individual substance, then, comprises matter and form. The example of a silver spoon allows us to say three things about a substance: first, it is an individual thing; second, it is a kind of thing (a spoon); and third, it has an individual existence of its own.

One way of telling whether something is a substance is to ask what it turns into when it ceases to exist: a rainbow, for example, does not turn into anything else when it disappears. It is not a substance but a phenomenon; you cannot collect any rainbow and store it in a tube, as you can drops of water.

I propose to consider substance under seven headings: first, how it is related to the central question of metaphysics; second, how it is part of ordinary grammar; third, its three meanings in Aristotle; fourth, how it is a cause of existence; fifth, why it is the first of existent things; sixth, criticisms of the idea of substance; and seventh, the value of this concept.

THE QUESTION OF BEING

Aristotle calls metaphysics "first philosophy", because it is about what exists. The idea that something exists is the first to come into our mind, because whatever else we say about a rose, for example, we first recognise that it exists or we would not think that we were talking about anything real. The existent, then, is the first of all things, because everything we affirm must exist in some way. Things exist in two ways: either by themselves or in other things. A silver spoon exists by itself; colours and surfaces, on the other hand, only exist *in* other things. A curve does not exist by itself, but something is curved. Whiteness does not exist on its own, but in white things, like white walls and white paper. Things that exist on their own come before things that only exist in other things, because the latter cannot exist without the former. The things that exist on their own are substances. Thus Aristotle says that first philosophy is about substance, because this is the *first of existent things*.[1] The question "What is being?" then reduces to the question "What is substance?"[2]

What exists in other things, we predicate of these things: for example, the paper is white, the spoon is curved. We predicate things of a subject; predicates need a subject. Thus, the Greek concept of substance is equivalent to our *subject*: a substance is a subject of qualities like white, curved, light, large, dense, luminous and so on. For us to be able to apply predicates like "is standing" and "is porous", the subject first has to *exist*. This is a substance. Thus first philosophy is about substance, because substance is the first of existent things.

THE CATEGORIES

The key to understanding Aristotle about substance is his doctrine of the ten categories. These are: substance, quality, quantity, position, time, stance or posture, relation, having, doing and having done to one. The categories tell us various ways in which things exist. There is a difference, however, between the first category and all the others, because we predicate all the others of the first category but we do not predicate substance of other things; it is the subject. To make this clearer, let us take as our subject the painter Paul Cézanne and predicate various things of him in each of the categories.

1	Substance	Cézanne
2	Quality (what sort?)	artistic
3	Quantity (how much?)	big
4	Position (where?)	at Aix-en-Provence
5	Time (when?)	in 1894

---

[1] Metaphysics Z VII c.1 1028a3O.
[2] Ibid. Z VII c.1 1028b3.

6	Stance (or posture)	sitting
7	Relation (to others)	younger than Manet
8	Having (possessing)	with a beard, with a hat
9	Doing (action)	painting
10	Having done to one (passion)	being shaded by a tree, being admired

At the head of the list we put substance and draw a line between this and all the other categories, because they are all about the first one. But there is one thing that we have so far left out; we have not said what the subject is. The most important thing about Cézanne is that he is a man. "Cézanne is a man" is not a statement of identity, but tells us what he is. To say that he is an artist or painter does not tell us what kind of being Cézanne is, because he would still be a human being if he were not a painter. Being a man is not a quality of Cézanne, as being genial is. You simply have not got a man in the world without human nature, but you can have a man without his being genial. A man is something existing in the world, but geniality is not anything on its own in the world. It is human beings that are genial. Thus substance serves two roles: it names a subject and tells us what it is as a whole. The kind it belongs to is its nature. These two meanings of substance (individual subject and nature), together with the modern meaning of material substance, give us Aristotle's three meanings of substance, for he says that it is in one way matter, in another essence, and in a third way an individual thing.

THE THREE MEANINGS OF SUBSTANCE

First, substance is *matter*. The word "substance" literally means what "stands under". The word used by Aristotle for substance in this sense is *hupokeimenon*, literally what "lies under". Matter especially seems to be substance in this sense, because we predicate quantity, shape, quality and the rest of matter. Matter also seems to be substance, because it is the *substrate* of change, as when a silver chalice is melted down and a plate is made out of the silver, or a chrysalis turns into a butterfly. Matter includes weight, measure, source of energy and shape. But substance is not just matter, because form also belongs to substance; so substance seems rather to be a compound of matter and form. Secondly, it is not necessary that an individual substance be material but only that it is *undivided in itself and divided from all others.*[3] There could, for instance, be immaterial substances. After all, mathematicians talk about "immaterial objects", but these objects of thought cannot exist on their own. As they are immaterial, they can only exist in something that is itself immaterial. Immaterial substances would be minds or intelligences.

As nothing is just its matter, for matter always exists with some definite form which makes it be *what* it is, Aristotle then considers the second meaning of substance.

Second, then, substance is *essence*. The essence of a thing is *what* it is. Something is a snail because it has the essence or nature of a snail; it is having this essence which makes it a snail. Having the snail nature marks a snail off from all other things without this nature. A snail has the "what it is to be" a snail. The what something is (*to ti estin*) is the primary sense of being (*to on*), Aristotle says, and this signifies substance.[4] We know a thing most of all, he says, when we know *what* it is. When I see a flower which I cannot identify, I want to know what kind of flower it is. The "what it is for something to be what it is" may be called the "whatness" of a thing. The word

---

[3] Ibid. Z VII c.3 1029a27.
[4] Ibid. Z VII c.1 1028a15.

"quiddity", from *quidditas*, literally means the "whatness" of something, although it is better to avoid abstract terms like "quiddity" as far as possible, and use words of ordinary language. Only *kinds* of thing have essences. Chopin would still have been the same kind of being even if he had not been musical; a human being is not musical by essence. What makes something be what it is, is also its substantial form. But nothing material or corporeal is just its form: I am not just my form or my soul.

So, we get a third meaning of substance. Substance is an individual thing or *suppositum*. In criticizing Plato's theory of the Forms, Aristotle remarks that the Horse Form does not beget a horse; instead, a whole horse, or rather two horses, beget a horse. So he says that in one way substance is matter and in another way it is essence, but in a third way it is the composite of matter and form, because a whole horse is generated by a whole horse, not just by the form of a horse. So the whole thing, consisting of matter and form, is the substance for Aristotle. Plato thought that the Forms alone were *the* beings, but Aristotle regards individual existent things as substances. A horse is something with matter and form, for a horse is by nature a body. So the third meaning of substance is a combination of the first two: it is the individual existent thing composed of matter and form.

Although individual substances are compounds of matter and form, a substance is not so much matter plus form as matter *with* a certain form. A chair is wood with or in a certain form, the form of a chair. There are two kinds of form: *substantial* and *accidental*. Natural things have substantial forms: this is to say, they cannot be what they are without this form. Accidental forms can vary without the matter ceasing to be the kind that it is. Every element has a substantial form which distinguishes it from every other kind of matter: chrome, nickel and platinum have substantial forms. Wood has a substantial form. But a chair has an accidental form, because its wood would still be wood even if it were not a chair; if the same wood were a table instead, it would still be the same kind of wood, say beech or ash. All living things have substantial forms, and artefacts accidental forms: copper is all the same copper whether it has the accidental form of a gong or of a pipe.

We have already remarked that things are either made by nature or by art. To make something is to bring it into existence. When something comes into existence, be it a box or a squirrel, it (a) comes *from* something (b) by the *agency* of something (c) to *be* something. *Matter* is what a material thing is made from. It is made what it is by its *form*. And it becomes something, an individual thing or *substance*. These are the three meanings of substance which we have just noted above. Nature itself can be an agent in making natural things: for example, an oak tree comes from an acorn by nature, but an oaken table comes from an oak tree by the art of a carpenter.

Things made by art come from an artificer or artist, for the forms of works of art first exist in the minds of their makers, who have an idea of what they are going to make. It is the same with inventors of machines and instruments. Aristotle says that when someone makes a bronze sphere, he does not make the matter or the form; these are given. What he does is to give to some bronze matter the form of a sphere.[5] We do not produce the essence, but something with an essence. A bronze sphere is made out of bronze which we find already existing, but where does the form come from, if we do not make or create it? One might say, from nature. But as the forms of things made by art come from the mind of

---

[5] Ibid. Z VII c.8 1033a30.

their maker, when nature produces things with distinct essences, as it does, for example, when a crocus produces a crocus, perhaps this is because nature too comes from a mind, which first thought of all its forms. As we have already noted, Hobbes called nature "the art of God".

In all production, Aristotle remarks, there is thinking and making in matter. When nature produces things with definite forms without thinking, this is because it comes from a mind which has thought of its forms. Nature that reproduces its forms seems to come from a mind, for form comes from *thought*. One might reply that nature does it by chance, but natural things would not reproduce things with the same form over and again by chance, for by chance they might produce anything. This makes it unlikely that nature has come about by chance. The wonderful structure of the human body seems to be more like a work of art than a product of mere chance.

A CAUSE OF EXISTENCE

Two of Aristotle's main points about substance are first, that substance is a cause of existence, and second, that it is "the first of existent things".[6] Whatever makes something be what it is, is a cause of its existence. Something is a substance, because it is one thing. A watch only exists when all its parts are united. So what makes it be one is also a cause of its existence. Things are not just their parts, because all the parts can exist separately without being one thing. So what makes them be one thing is something else besides their parts. Nothing is just its parts, for you can have the parts without having the thing they make; I can have the parts of a clock without the clock. Substance is a cause of existence, because

---

[6] Ibid. Z VII c.1 1028a30.

unless the parts are one individual thing, such as a clock, a clock does not exist. We count a clock as an individual thing or item existing in the world.

Another thing which makes the parts be a substance, Aristotle says, is their purpose.[7] What makes a collection of wheels and springs be a clock, is that it is for telling the time. What makes the parts of a bicycle be what they are, is that they are a means of transport for the rider. To take Aristotle's example, what makes stones and timbers be a house, which is a substance, is their purpose: to provide a shelter for human beings to live in. The same stones or bricks could be used for a different purpose: for example, to make a wall, which is for enclosing a field or marking a boundary. You cannot have a wall without stones or bricks, but stones and bricks do not by themselves make a wall or a house; so what makes them into a wall or house is something else — their form. What makes steel into a knife is that it is for cutting or peeling; its form is adapted to its purpose.

A good analogy, first used by Plato, for parts making a whole, is a syllable.[8] A syllable is a unit consisting of letters in a certain pattern or form. A letter is an element of a syllable, and a word is an element of a sentence. A syllable may be compared with a substance, and its letters with its parts or constituent elements. The word "element" itself comes from combining three successive letters of the alphabet: l,m,n. A syllable is more than its parts, because the same parts or elements can be used to make different syllables. For instance, the four letters a,b,d and r, make two quite different words in English: "drab" (dull) and "bard" (a poet). So what makes the parts be a syllable or substance is something else besides them,

---

[7] Ibid. Z VII c.17 1041a3O.
[8] Theaetetus 202b.

because the same elements can be used to make a different syllable or substance.

The molecules which build material things are like the syllables which build words. Chemists represent elements by letters, which they write together to represent the elements that constitute a molecule: for example, a molecule of copper sulphide is written as Cu_2S. Molecules consist of chemical elements arranged in certain configurations, as syllables consist of letters in a certain pattern. Molecules can also be varied by adding or taking away one or other of their elements. For instance, if you take one atom of copper from copper sulphide and then add four atoms of oxygen, you get copper sulphate ($CuSO_4$). Then replace the atom of copper with two of potassium and you get potassium sulphate (K_2SO_4). These signs are like pictures of molecules. As syllables are not just their letters, for the same letters can be used to make different syllables, so things are not just their material constituents. Nor, therefore, is matter the sole cause of things. The physicist Schrödinger even says that material things are more form than matter: the ultimate particles of matter are, as it were, "pure shape".[9]

A fish is not just its parts (its fins, gills, scales and bones); rather a fish is what they are parts of. We cannot talk about things as parts unless they are parts of something, that is of an individual substance. A fish is an individual substance. What makes the parts or elements be one thing cannot be one of the elements, or else we would just remain on the level of elements. So it must be something else besides them; Aristotle says it is substance.[10] Thus substance is a cause of existence, since it is the cause of the elements existing as an individual thing. We see that the parts only have existence as a whole,

[9] *Nature and the Greeks: Science and Humanism p.125.*
[10] Metaphysics Z VII c.17 1041b2O.

especially in living things, for the parts of an animal or plant cease to preserve their form or to have their function apart from the living whole.

What a thing is, is not just its elements, but what it is as a whole. A tree for example, is not just a collection of roots, a trunk, branches and leaves; there is something that they are as a whole, because they have a natural unity, namely a tree. As Wittgenstein remarks, when I see a tree, I do not just see a lot of parts but I see the parts as one thing.[11] A tree is what the roots, trunk, branches and leaves are. What a thing is, Aristotle says, is the primary meaning of substance. So it is substance which makes the parts exist as an individual thing. In living things, the parts have no existence of their own except as one living thing. When a finger is removed from the body, it keeps the shape of a finger if it is preserved artificially; otherwise it decays. It has no independent existence of its own.

THE FIRST OF EXISTENT THINGS

This now helps us to answer the question: "Why does Aristotle call substance 'the first of existent things'?" First, a substance is like a subject. Many things do not exist except *in* subjects: for example, shapes, surfaces and colours. Secondly, substance is what makes the parts or elements exist as an individual thing: it makes bricks be a house or a wall, which are two different sorts of substance. Thirdly, unless things were substances, they would have no individual existence of their own but would all be parts of one great substance or mass of matter, as some of the Presocratic philosophers thought. But we recognise that things have their own existence, for one thing can go out of existence without other

---

[11] *Philosophical Investigations* I 47.

things around it losing their existence too. Things have individual existence, and what makes them individual is being substances. Thus, substance is the first of existent things, because unless things were substances, we would not have many individual things with their own existence, such as clocks and bicycles; they would just be modifications of one great thing, the world.

Unless we talk of things as substances, we cannot talk of their *coming into* and *going out of* existence. This is what the ancient and mediæval writers called the *generation* and *corruption* of things. Unless things can be said to come into and go out of existence, they are just alterations here and there on the surface of one great mass of matter, without having individual existence. This was the view of Spinoza (1632-1677), who thought that everything was a material or mental modification of a single substance. It makes sense, however, to talk of things coming into and going out of existence, for when an artist produces a picture there is one new item in the world, and when a sparrow falls to the ground there is one less bird existing in the world. When a tree is felled, something certainly goes out of existence. If things go out of existence, they can also come into existence. This is still more true of human beings than of pictures; we know that what is conceived has a distinct life and, therefore, individual existence. When a human being comes into existence, a quite new individual with its own identity exists in the world. There is not just an alteration of previously existing matter.

Things are substances, because they have an independent existence. To see whether things are substances, we may ask whether Lot's wife was the same substance as the pillar of salt she turned into.[12] When we consider that coral is a

---

[12] Genesis 19:26.

different substance from the marine creatures that turn into it, the pillar of salt was not the same substance as Lot's wife, because salt is a different substance from a human being. A pillar of salt came into existence in place of a human being, who ceased to exist by a change.

Aristotle distinguishes between *change* and *alteration*. A change goes deeper than an alteration. It is alteration when something changes in some aspect but remains an individual of the same kind. For example, an alteration occurs when the grey feathers of a young flamingo turn pink, for the flamingo does not change its nature. But a change occurs when we get a new substance, or a substance ceases to have the same essence, as when an amethyst is changed into a yellow substance through being heated. *What* a thing is as a whole is the primary meaning of substance, Aristotle says (his second meaning). Change is of substantial form, alteration of an accidental form. When feathers or leaves change colour, this is a change of accidental form, that is an alteration, for the individual thing retains its substantial form, as it does not change its nature of being a bird or a tree. A bird or tree is also the subject of this change of colour. But when copper is changed into another substance by the addition of another element, a change occurs; it becomes a new substance. When, however, copper turns green, this is an alteration; but when it turns into copper sulphate by the addition of sulphur, there is a substantial change. A change, as distinct from an alteration, is a change of something *as a whole*. When a tree is turned into charcoal by lightning, a change occurs, for a tree is a living thing, but charcoal does not live or act like a tree.

CRITICISMS OF SUBSTANCE

In modern times, however, the idea of substance has been much criticized, beginning with John Locke (1632-1704). We notice two tendencies among those who undermine it: either to say that things are collections of qualities or that they merely consist of appearances (phenomena).

For Locke, all our ideas either come from sensible objects or from the mind's internal reflection on its own working. Qualities, he says, are the powers of objects to produce sensible ideas in us, such as of heat and cold, by affecting us. Being brittle, luminous, opaque, magnetic, solid, coloured and soluble, are qualities of bodies. We notice that, for Locke, the senses "let in" ideas, whereas ideas for Plato are only apprehended by the intellect. Locke divides the qualities which produce ideas in us into two groups: primary and secondary qualities. This distinction had already been made by Galileo. Primary qualities are size, shape, number, motion, position and weight; however much you divide a material body, every part has all these qualities. Primary qualities are the ones studied by physics and are objective. Secondary qualities are sound, colour, taste and how an object is to the sense of touch; they are subjective; we cannot measure them exactly in the same way as primary qualities. As qualities do not exist on their own, but in things, Locke says that sensible qualities exist in a substratum which supports them. We call this substratum "substance". But a substance does not itself consist of any qualities, because it is what has them, Locke says. If it consisted of qualities, he thought, it could not be the subject that has them. So substance becomes the unknowable support of sensible qualities; it is an "I know not what", says Locke.[13] A substance-term just expresses some set of co-existing

---

[13] *An Essay concerning Human Understanding* II c.23, 2 and 14.

qualities. As certain sets of qualities are united in one subject, we give then one name, and the names of substances are the names of collections of simple ideas. Coloured glass has one set of qualities, mahogany wood another set.

There are two common ways of thinking about substance. One is that substance is what you get by stripping away all its qualities. The other is that it entirely consists of qualities. The first view was held by Locke, the second by Hume. Locke, however, did not, like Hume, say that substances are just collections of qualities, but that the *names* of substances are the names of sets of sensible qualities, for he thought that substance is the substrate which supports them, although it is not anything knowable in itself. Aristotle, on the other hand, did not get to substance by peeling away the outer layers of qualities, but made substance the subject of which we predicate qualities.

Locke was unable to show how we get from the ideas of sensible qualities that bodies produce in us to real things. For, if all we directly know is our ideas or sense-impressions, how do we know that they are of anything real? As Locke divided the world of ideas from the external world, without any means of bridging the two, George Berkeley (1685-1753), the Anglican bishop of Cloyne, took the next step of deleting Locke's world of unknowable things and only retaining ideas. So Berkeley denied the existence of matter and said that things consist of ideas. What is immediately known is an idea for Berkeley; "Idea is now commonly used by philosophers to denote the immediate objects of the understanding". As what we immediately know are ideas, things just consist of ideas. Berkeley admitted the existence of some substances, however; these were immaterial substances or spirits, because ideas only exist in minds. Ideas do not exist on their own, but only when thought or perceived by someone. Berkeley, then, kept

Locke's ideas; Hume likewise did away with Locke's unknowable substrate but kept his qualities instead.

As a substance is an "I know not what" for Locke, David Hume (1711-1776) concluded that substance is a fiction, calling it an "unintelligible chimera".[14] Objects, for Hume, are nothing but bundles of qualities or characteristics. The key to understanding Hume is his axiom that all our ideas are derived from impressions. As we do not have an impression of substance, but only of sensible qualities, the idea of substance is not of anything real. The only existences we know are our perceptions, and we have no idea of anything except of our perceptions, but perceptions are quite different from substances. It follows for Hume that substances are just collections of qualities, because "We have no idea of substance distinct from ideas of particular qualities."[15] Ideas of bodies are nothing but collections of ideas formed by the mind of distinct qualities, which have constant union one with another.[16] It should be remarked that, if things are just collections of qualities, nothing is really one; they do not have an essential unity, nor is there anything they are *as a whole*. But the reason why things have properties, or qualities, is that they are a certain kind of substance. For example, gold has the properties of being malleable and durable.

Hume's criticism of substance, however, is itself open to various criticisms. First, if things just consist of their qualities, we do not predicate qualities of a subject but of one another. As Aristotle remarks, we do not say that musical is white or white is musical but a human being is white and musical. Being a man or human is not a quality of a human being but is what he or she is as a whole and essentially. Things are no more the

---

[14] *A Treatise of Human Nature* I iv 5.

[15] Ibid. I i 6.

[16] Ibid. I iv 3.

sum of their qualities or properties than a syllable is just the sum of its letters. The reason why a lot of qualities are related one to another is that they are all related to one thing, a substance, which gives them their unity. A fish, which is an individual substance, is not just its parts but it is what they are all parts of.

Second, as Hume does away with substance, and only retains the qualities, he has a difficulty in explaining the identity of things when their appearances change. How, for example, do we know that the bright shapes seen in the sky on successive nights, which vary from a crescent to a full round disc are all of the same object, the moon? Without this we cannot know that things continue to exist. Hume attempted to answer this by saying that the constancy of impressions, for example of the same person I see every day, gives the notion of continued existence. As the changes of an object are only gradual and quite imperceptible, he says, we readily pass from one idea to another in succession as though they are of one continuous thing.

Hume's qualities were replaced in the thought of Immanuel Kant (1724-1804) by appearances. Kant maintained that all we know of things is their appearances or *phenomena*; we never reach "the thing in itself" (*Ding an sich*), because you cannot think of a substance without its characteristics. Although Kant thought that we never know the substance but only its appearances, that is the *phenomena*, he required the idea of substance in order to explain the unity of a thing's phenomena and its *permanent* existence. Beneath the changing phenomena, Kant supposed that there were things with a continued existence, although he did not think we can know them in themselves.

Bertrand Russell (1872-1970), however, denied the continuous existence of things altogether; like Hume, he thought that we just have "the illusion of persistence". Russell consequently makes all talk of the identity of things superfluous, for he holds that what we perceive as the same object is really a series of momentary objects. Although Russell speaks of "all the familiar objections to the notion of substance"[17], he seems not to have realised the difficulties of his own view.

For example, Russell holds that I am not really the same man, but a series of momentary men, although I appear to be a continuous individual, just as what gives the impression of a continuous picture on the screen in the cinema really consists of a series of isolated pictures shown in rapid succession.[18] Russell's analogy of a film, however, can be turned against him, for when we ask why the series of pictures can appear as a continuous picture, we see that this is only possible because they all belong to *one* thing, the strip of film on the spool, which is like a substance. How could one take successive pictures of a man rolling down a hill, for example, so that they appear to be of one thing rolling down the hill, unless they *are* of one and the same thing? If we were really a lot of momentary beings, our actions would not be continuous or appear to be so, but jerky.

For Russell, objects are just groups of sensible qualities, which he calls *sensibilia*; wholes are logical constructions, he says, but nothing real. Russell presents a combination of Berkeley and Hume: as all we immediately perceive of things is "sense-data", which is Russell's name for Berkeley's ideas, so material things just consist of sense-data. The view that things just consist of their appearances is known as *phenomenalism*. More will be said about phenomenalism in Chapter Eleven.

---

[17] *An Inquiry into Meaning and Truth* (1940; Penguin, 1962), p.92.
[18] "The Ultimate Constituents of Matter", *Mysticism and Logic* (1916; Allen & Unwin, 1973), p.96.

Things cannot just be phenomena, for phenomena do not act; it is a *subject* that acts. Matter for Russell ceases to be anything solid, and is "a series of events in space-time". For a similar view held by a physicist, one may turn to Erwin Schrödinger, who said that particles are events, because we cannot know that it is the same particle that reappears. Particles now are thought of as points of mass and energy.[19] The view that the world consists of events rather than things will be discussed in Chapter Six, when we come to consider existence. Here it is enough to remark that events are actions, and actions only come about by *things* acting. Whatever particles may be, we shall never get matter if the smallest units of matter are not material, but merely events or "pure shape". If matter exists, the units out of which it is made must also be material.

REASONS FOR SUBSTANCE

We require the idea of substance for several reasons. Unless things are substances, there is nothing they are essentially. If there is nothing they are essentially, everything predicated of them is accidental. But we do not predicate being a man of the painter Cézanne accidentally, as we do being bearded: it is what he is as a whole. What something is as a whole is answered by the first of the ten categories: substance. Unless there is something that an individual is as a whole, it is not one thing at all, but just a collection of parts. So substance also explains the unity of a thing.

We have seen that things are more than just the sum of their parts, for in the case of artefacts like watches, they only exist when their parts are given unity, and with living things,

---

[19] *Nature and the Greeks. Science and Humanism* (1954; Cambridge, 1996), p.121.

the parts only exist as long as they are united with the whole. The leg of a horse, for example, only exists as a leg as long as it is attached to a living horse. Thus living things have an *essential* unity. And everything only exists as long as it is *one* being: a watch, for example, only exists as long as its parts are united. Thus we also need the idea of substance to explain the identity of things, and with identity their continuity of existence, for it is the *same* thing which continues to exist, whatever accidental changes or alterations it may undergo. There is no identity without unity.

As Elizabeth Anscombe has pointed out, our natural way of speaking recognises that substances really exist, for one of the common ways of describing things is to use the names of substances. We may say of something "It looked like leather", or "It felt like silk", or "It is furry." Leather, silk and fur are substances. Again, the answer to the question, "What is platinum?" is, "A metal". Metals are substances.[20]

In summary, we may first say that the question of what being is, is the question of what substance is, because substance is the first of existent things. Second, a substance is the subject of predicates. Third, the primary meaning of substance is what a thing *is*. When we say that Cézanne is a man, this is in the first category of substance. Fourth, there is something that things are as *wholes*; they are not just their elements or parts or qualities. Fifth, substance is what makes them be what they are. Thus, it is a cause of their existence. As substance is a cause of the existence of things, our next topic should be existence.

---

[20] *Collected Philosophical Papers* (Blackwell, 1981), Vol. II, p.41.

Chapter Five

EXISTENCE

The idea of existence goes with everything we talk about; whatever we talk about, we either think it exists in reality, or not. We say that all sorts of things exist: for example, the British Museum, the British Academy and the British constitution. But they do not all exist in the same way. You can point to a building with a classical front in London and say, "That is the British Museum", and tell others how to find it. But you cannot similarly point to the British Academy, except in so far as it uses a particular building as its premises, for it is an association of scholars, whose members change over the years. The British constitution cannot be found anywhere, since it is unwritten; yet it exists, for it has been handed on and it is possible to state exactly what it is. It seems, then, at least to exist in the minds of people who agree about its contents.

I shall begin by considering six different kinds of thing, about which there is a question as to whether they can be said to exist. I shall then discuss, second, the three uses of the verb "is"; third, the two meanings of "being" in Aquinas; fourth, existence according to Frege and Russell; and fifth, the distinction between essence and existence.

VARIETIES OF EXISTENCE

First, then, the Equator seems to exist, for it is something quite definite that everyone agrees about. You can cross the Equator, yet when you cross it you do not see any line on the ground or in the ocean. So if it is a line, it is not a real line. Does this mean that it is imaginary or fictitious, if it is not a real thing? It cannot be purely imaginary, because it is not the invention of someone's imagination. But you might say that it is an imaginary line, because you do not see a line round the earth. What then is the Equator? It is all those points of the surface of the earth that are equidistant between the North and South Poles. Did the Equator exist before someone thought up its definition? We may compare the Equator with another line, the Berlin Wall. The Equator is not a visible object like the Berlin Wall; nor can you dismantle the Equator, as the Berlin Wall was dismantled in 1989. So, although the Berlin Wall was more real than the Equator when it existed, the Equator still exists but the Berlin Wall no longer does so. How is it that what is an imaginary line remains in existence?

Second, rainbows exist, in that they can be seen at any time; given the right conditions, there can always be a rainbow. But rainbows only exist for a short time and the same rainbow never exists again; it is always a different rainbow. But do rainbows exist at all — that is, are they real things? As we have seen in an earlier chapter, you cannot keep a piece of rainbow. They are not made out of anything, nor do they turn into anything when they disappear. So they are not substances. Yet they seem to be quite real, for you can study them scientifically and even photograph them. What then is a rainbow? It is a *phenomenon*, an appearance, which comes into existence when the viewer faces clouds with the sun directly behind him. The source of light and drops of water in the cloud or spray of a fountain are the real things; the rainbow is an *effect* of light on drops of water. It is only an effect; it does not cause anything.

Third, the Ninth Symphony of Beethoven seems to exist and not to exist. It is a piece of music, and music consists of sounds. So a symphony only seems to exist when it is actually being played. But how could it be played by anyone unless it already existed, for it is not composed each time that it is played? Unless it exists, it is not there for anyone to play; but it can be performed at any time. Where does it exist when it is not being played? Surely, in the notes written in a book of music. But the marks in the book are only signs of the sounds to be produced by players with their instruments. We could say that the printed notes give the form, or pattern, of the sound which can be made to exist. Yet a symphony seems to exist all the time once it has been composed, and not just when it is being played, unless it is lost. It still exists in books when it is not in people's minds. Does this mean that the Ninth Symphony is an idea, if it still exists when it is not being played? It is a piece of music and music is made with sounds, but an idea is not a sound. A musician first has to have an idea of what he or she is going to produce in the medium of sound, as a sculptor does of what he is going to produce in stone. The difference is that a statue exists without interruption once the idea has been realised in its medium, but Beethoven's idea can be realised every time that players follow his idea as it is recorded in copies of his score.

Fourth, we may think of another thing for which we use signs: numbers. Are numbers real objects? On the one hand, they do not seem to be subjective ideas, for we do not each have our own different ideas of numbers. They have quite definite properties, which no one can alter. So they are objective and seem to be like objects. There are two reasons for this. One is that we talk about *the* number four, as though it were a definite object. Numerals are the names of objects, numbers. We also say that "The number of stars in the Great Bear is seven", as though there were an identity between seven and a number. Also, we do not get the ideas of numbers, as we get other ideas, by abstracting them. I get my idea of stars from seeing many stars, but I do not get the idea of seven in the same way from seven stars, for seven is not the property of any one of those seven stars. As numbers are not the properties of individual things, except in the case of one, they seem to be independent objects. They also seem to be objects, because we can do things with numbers, even with the number "nought", which has proved to be a most useful number in mathematics.

So the German mathematician and philosopher, Gottlob Frege (1848-1925), said that numbers are self-standing objects (*selbständige Gegenstände*), but not actual objects. They are not actual objects (they are not *wirklich*), because they do not act. They are unchanging in themselves; you can only do things *with* them, not *to* them. *Wirklich* is the German for real; it is connected with the verb *wirken*, to work or act. To say that something is *wirklich* is like saying it is actual. Numbers for Frege, then, are non-actual objects.[1] Numerals are signs of objects, but numbers are not physical objects; you will not find them anywhere in the universe by looking for them. So are they immaterial objects like Plato's Forms, as several well-known mathematicians of this century have been quite

---

[1] *Foundations of Arithmetic (Grundlagen)* 57.

prepared to think?[2] If they are immaterial objects, they must at least be objects of the mind, even if they do not exist as independent objects like Plato's Forms. The American logician, W.V.O. Quine, says that "Abstract objects have long since proved indispensable to natural science", and names numbers as being such things.[3]

On the other hand, we may want to say that numerals do not name objects, because Frege says that numbers apply to *concepts* rather than objects. So objects do not have numbers, but concepts do, because we count the number of objects that come under a concept. To count things, I first have to decide what sort of things I am going to count, which is to select a concept under which I am going to count them: for instance, the number of geraniums in the greenhouse or the number of moons of Jupiter. Numbers, then, seem to belong to concepts rather than objects, because the same objects can be counted with different numbers: a hundred soldiers are one century, two shoes are one pair. It seems to be contradictory, however, to say that numbers are objects but that they apply to concepts. Do we not rather apply concepts to things? Numbers may seem to be objects, because objects can be counted; we can count the number of numbers of a kind, for example, prime numbers or square numbers less then 99.

Fifthly, we may wonder whether, if numbers seem to be objects of the mind rather than self-standing objects, our *thoughts* exist? We can count thoughts like objects. They also seem to be objects, because we can pass them on to others by communicating them. Unlike material objects, when I hand over a thought to someone else it can also still exist in my mind; but when I hand over a hammer to someone else, it

---

[2] E.g. G.H. Hardy and R. Penrose; cf. the latter's *The Emperor's New Mind* (Vintage, 1990) p.126.

[3] *The Pursuit of Truth* (Harvard, 1992) p.25.

cannot remain in my hand any longer. Thoughts also seem to be objects with an independent existence, because the theorems of mathematics, like Pythagoras' theorem, may be timelessly true; that is, they always were true, even before anyone thought of them, for what Pythagoras noticed about the properties of right-angled triangles was true of them before he expressed his theorem.

On the other hand, thoughts do not exist like objects in the room. If I were to make an inventory of things in my room, thoughts would not be included among them. When I am sitting in a mediæval chapel, I know that the walls I am looking at did not exist just three minutes, but also seven hundred years ago. But where are the thoughts that I was having three minutes ago? These no longer exist as the walls did three minutes ago. Yet I and many others can have the same thought that Galileo had about the oscillation of a pendulum. So it seems that this thought in some way still exists.

We have to distinguish between the *content* and the *occurrence* of a thought. I can have the same thought as Galileo about the oscillation of a pendulum because the content of my thought is the same as the thought expressed in his law about pendulums taking the same time to swing through any arc. But obviously my thought is not Galileo's thought; for one thing, I am thinking now, over four hundred years after Galileo had his thought one day in 1582, as he watched a lamp swinging inside Pisa Cathedral. So the *occurrence* of the thought in me and in Galileo differs. The occurrence of a thought is an *event*. Thoughts are not so much things, as *of* things; they do not exist on their own but *in* minds.

Sixth, we may consider whether *events* exist. Wittgenstein begins his *Tractatus* by declaring that the world is the totality of facts (*Tatsachen*), not of things (*Dinge*). The Battle of Agincourt was an event. It is also a fact that there was a battle at Agincourt in 1415. Does the world consist of facts like objects? One reason for saying that it does is that the state of the world at any time, which is how it *really* is, is due to events. But what are events? Are they like objects or real things? Let us take an example of an event: a duel is an event. A duel consists of two fencers crossing the swords and, possibly, hitting one another with their swords. The same two fencers and pair of swords can exist without there being any duel, as they do before and after the duel. So they do not make the event of a duel by themselves. The event comes about by the fencers and swords being in a certain *relation* to each other. When this relation ceases, so does the event; it is then past. An eclipse is also an event: it comes into existence by the juxtaposition of three things — the sun, the moon and the earth in a straight line, with the moon or the earth between the sun and the other.

Events are transitory, but the actors in the event continue to exist. Moreover, no event comes about without some actor *causing* it. The actor, or agent, of an event may be a piece of matter: a flood is an event, and one of its agents is a great quantity of water breaking its confines. So things are prior to events, because events come about by things getting into new relations with one another. The world primarily consists of *things* rather than events and facts. Events involve changes in the world, and changes presuppose subjects of change. Facts are how the things exist; there is no fact without them existing, except a negative one, such as that there are no hippopotamuses in the river Thames.

THE THREE USES OF "IS"

Existence and essence make a pair of terms. Essence tells us *what* something is, existence *that* it exists. To say "Chimeras are beasts" only tells us what chimeras are; it does not tell us whether any such animals exist. From this we see that we use the word "is" in at least two ways: as the *copula* with a predicate ("A flamingo is pink" or "A whale is a mammal"); and as the "is" of *existence* ("There is a wood on the hill", or "There is a lighthouse on the rock"). The "is" of existence is used on its own; it does not join a predicate with a subject, as in the first use. Perhaps this second use is best seen in the negative statement, "Joseph is no more, Simeon is no more";[4] that is, they no longer exist.

There is also a third use of "is", the "is" of *identity*, when two nouns name one and the same object: for example, "Mercury is the nearest planet to the sun", or "The Morning Star is Venus." What "Morning Star" and "Venus" name is an identical object. But in "Venus is a planet", we have the "is" of the copula, because we predicate "planet" of Venus, and say what sort of thing Venus is, just as a whale is a mammal.

EXISTENCE AND BEING

Bertrand Russell distinguished between a broad and narrow sense of being.[5] A being in the broad sense, for Russell, is every possible object of thought. Anything that can be counted is a being. Chimeras are beings, but they do not exist. So not every being has existence or is a being in the narrower sense. Only things that have actual existence are beings in the narrower sense; existence only belongs to some beings. Some

---

[4] Genesis 42:36.
[5] *The Principles of Mathematics* (1903) c. VI paragraph 72.

things do not exist on their own or by themselves; other beings only exist in the mind. We might call them "beings of the mind" (*entia rationis*); perhaps numbers are like this. Russell thought it necessary to distinguish between being and existence like this, so that we can deny the existence of things; otherwise, if what we are talking about is simply nothing, it cannot even be said not to exist. We are back to our opening question of the first chapter: how can we say what Pegasus is, if he is not? Hence, Russell says that we need the concept of being for what does not exist. Russell's distinction between the broad and narrow sense of being roughly corresponds with Aquinas' two meanings of *ens* (being). Not everything which we say "is" also exists.

THE TWO MEANINGS OF BEING

St. Thomas Aquinas (1225-1274) distinguishes between two ways of talking about being (*ens*): the being which corresponds to something *real* and of which we can predicate the ten categories (substance, quality, relation, action etc.), and also the being which is *true* of things, although it may not be anything in itself.[6] This use of "being" signifies the truth of a proposition, although it may not refer to anything that really exists.

Aquinas illustrates the difference between the two meanings of "being" with the example of blindness. As some animals and humans are blind, we talk about there being blindness. Thus blindness in some sense has being, because there are some beings which are blind. Blindness has being in the second sense, because it is true to say that some people are blind. But it does not have being in the first sense, because

---

[6] *De ente et essentia* c.1; *Summa theologiae* I q. 48, 2 ad 2.

blindness is not anything real. The words "real" and "reality" come from *res*, the Latin for thing. Blindness is not a "thing", because it does not put into, or add anything to, a being; rather it detracts from the being of something.

We do not call everything that cannot see blind, but only those things which by nature are meant to have sight; we do not call stones blind, because they are not missing anything from their being by not having sight, although they may have a lower level of being than things whose nature it is to see. But human beings miss something from their proper and complete being when they lack the power of sight. Thus blindness is the lack or absence of something. It is in this sense that it is not anything real.

Sight, on the other hand, is something real (a reality or *res*), because it puts something into animals and human beings. It contributes to our being and existence, so that we have a fuller way of being than stones. Seeing is an activity that adds to our way of existing; blindness is the lack of this activity and so of one of the ways we exist. Although blindness is only a being in the second sense of *ens*, the things which are blind have being in the first sense; they have real existence. Blindness is not a being like sight in the first sense of being, because to say that someone is blind is rather to say that something does not exist in the eye, namely the power of sight. Blindness is only real in that it is true to say that some people are blind; but it is not a reality in itself, because it is the *absence* of something, namely of sight. It does not add to existence but takes away from our full existence. To say that blindness is really not anything existent is not to say that people are not really blind, for we truly predicate "blind" of some people. The ten categories are ways that things exist, but blindness is not a way of existing; rather it is a way of not existing by not having the activity of seeing.

SUBSTANTIAL AND ACCIDENTAL EXISTENCE

A being either exists by itself (*per se*) or by coming to something else (*per accidens*). Thus beings either exist *in* subjects or are subjects. What exists by itself is a substance. Thus Aquinas says that everything is called a being (*ens*), in the first sense of being, by its *substantial* existence.[7] Being means that something exists, rather than being only potential — what can be, but is not. For example, a penny has substantial existence. It is also potentially corroded or bent, in that it could be corroded or bent, although it is not yet so.

In Aquinas' view, the first idea that comes into our mind about anything is that it *exists*; whatever else we say about it, for instance that it is large, heavy, or bright, we grasp that it is a being or else we would not think that what we say were true of it. Thus, the idea of truth and being go together. A thing has as much truth as it has being, he says.[8]

We talk about things as "objects". The words "subject" and "object" have undergone a reversal of meaning. Subject is now mostly applied to the perceiver. We say, "That is how things seem to me 'subjectively'." But subject originally meant what we now call the *object*. For instance, if something that is really blue seems black to me, I say that it is "subjectively" black, although it is "objectively" blue. But in the original way of speaking, the blue thing is the subject of being blue and it is also an object *of* my perception or thought. Things were subjects in themselves and objects of the mind. A subject has substantial existence and we predicate the other nine categories of it. The categories are ways of speaking about the subject and specify further ways in which it exists. For example, to recall our example of Cézanne, he was gentle

---

[7] *Summa* I 5, 1 ad 1.
[8] Ibid. I 16, 3 *sed contra*.

(quality), lived in Aix (place) in the nineteenth century (time), wore a beard and hat, and painted (action). Cézanne had substantial existence as a man. What made him a human being was his substantial form. Many of the things we say about him were accidental to him; they could have been otherwise without his ceasing to have substantial existence as a human being. For example, it is not accidental to my nature that I have eyes and ears, for it is part of human nature to have these; but whether my eyes are blue or brown is accidental. An accident is what comes *to* something; the thing is the subject of it.

ACTUAL EXISTENCE

Aquinas defines existence as "the actuality of every form or nature".[9] A form or nature are what things *can* have or be; by themselves, they are potential. They are the sorts of things that something can be, and they receive existence in an individual. Something may be a horse or a zebra; horses and zebras are two sorts that animals can be. Other things may be lead or gold. What makes something *be* a horse or a zebra, lead or gold, is its form. The horse form in itself is potential; it is given *actual* existence in a horse. Thus existence is the actuality of every form or nature. Matter has to exist in some or other form. A new penny is potentially corrodible and may later become actually corroded. Things only exist as some kind of thing: metal must be steel or tin or one of the kinds of metal; a bird must be a corncrake or a partridge or one of the other definite kinds of bird. Steel is potentially a sword or a knife, because it can receive the form of a sword or knife. A sword exists when steel is given the form of a sword; that is, the

---

[9] *Summa theologiae* I 3, 4; 4, 1 ad 3; 50, 2 ad 3.

sword form is actualised in some steel. What makes things exist as the particular kind of thing that they are is their *form*. Nothing exists as a horse unless it has the form of a horse. Thus existence goes with form, because form makes things be what they are. Without form they would not exist as what they are, but be something else; there would, say, be a zebra rather than a horse.

The word "actual" comes from the Latin *actus*, an action or activity. Things can only exist on their own if they have some activity of their own; substances either act or are acted upon, that is, react.[10] Thus we talk about things "actually" existing as distinct from being potential. Potential things do not yet exist. Aquinas says that existence is the actuality of an essence, and action is the actuality of a power.[11] I have the power of sight, but I do not actually see when I am asleep or close my eyes. Only things that act or are acted upon have actual existence. Thoughts are not actual; they do not act. Whether they have an effect depends on the will and activity of the one who thinks them. Thought itself is an activity, which actualises the power of the mind.

A PROPERTY OF CONCEPTS

For Frege and Russell, who were both mathematicians, existence is not the actuality of things but a property of concepts. As we have already seen, we count things under a concept, because we first have to decide how we are going to count them. Is it, for instance, the number of bears or the number of elephants in the zoo? To say that something exists is to say that there is something which comes under a concept:

---

[10] This definition goes back to Plato, Sophist 247d-e.

[11] *Summa* I 54, 1.

to say that there are four bears is to say that four things fall under the concept of a bear.

Thus, Frege says that numbers belong to concepts rather than to things.[12] In his view, existence is denial of the number "nought".[13] So existence is the property of a concept, because it says that a concept is not empty, but has at least one thing falling under it. Conversely, to say that Venus has no moons is to say that nothing existent comes under the concept "moon of Venus", and to say that there are four corners of the earth is to say that four things come under the concept "corner of the earth".

Existence is the instantiation of a concept for Frege, as it is the instantiation of a form for Aquinas. A bear is an instance of the bear nature: the form of a bear is instantiated in every bear. Likewise, human beings are instantiations of human nature. Existence is the property of a concept for Frege, because to say that something exists is to say that the concept of it is instantiated so many times, and therefore numbers do not apply to things but to concepts. On Frege's view, "There is an even prime number" does not predicate "exist" of anything, but says that something comes under the concept of "even prime number". Thus existence is about the realisation of concepts in things for Frege. It seems, however, that existence first applies to things rather than concepts, because it is *things* which are actual. Concepts are not actual. They do not act; rather they are actualised by existent things.

But this does not mean that existence is a property of things, if it is not a property of concepts. It is not a property of things, because existence does not come into the definition of things or add to the description of what they are. Existence has to do with whether or not it is true *that* they are, as essence

---

[12] *Foundations of Arithmetic* 48.
[13] Ibid. 53.

does with *what* they are. As Aristotle once remarks, it is not part of the definition of anything that there is such a thing.[14] It is not part of the definition of a lion that there are any lions, or of a unicorn that unicorns exist. We distinguish, then, between existence and essence. Whether or not dodos now exist makes no difference to the concept of what a dodo is. Its definition is just the same now that they are extinct as it was when dodos existed. Wittgenstein, too, remarks that reality is not a property of things, which belongs to real but not to unreal horses, for there are no such things as unreal horses.[15]

ESSENCE AND EXISTENCE

There is a *real* difference between the essence and existence of a thing, between *what* it is and that *by which* it is, because many things can share the same nature but they do not share the same existence. All camels have the same nature, but every camel has its own separate existence; this is what makes a camel individual and divided from all other camels. Copernicus was a human being and Kepler also was a human being; thus they shared the same nature, but they did not share the same existence. As both had human nature, but Copernicus was not Kepler, that by which Copernicus was human and that by which he was this particular human being differed. He was human by his nature and form, but he was this particular man because human nature was instantiated in him with his individual existence. Copernicus and Kepler were the same in respect of their human nature, though each was an individual instance of this nature, and they differed in their existence.

---

[14] *Posterior Analytics* B 92b14.
[15] *Philosophical Remarks* 96.

John Duns Scotus (1265-1308), however, rejected this difference between that *by which* someone is human and *is* this particular human being. He said that everyone has what he called "thisness" (*haeccitas*), because an essence only has existence in this and that particular individual. Scotus argued that, since essence is only real if it exists, there is no distinction between essence and existence in reality; it is only a "formal" distinction in our minds. This would mean that we can only talk about the human nature of this and that person. For Copernicus to be human is the same as for him to be *this* human being, in Scotus' view.

But unless that by which people are human and are this particular human beings differ, we cannot talk about them sharing the same nature or, therefore, call them by the same name. We call things by the same name, because they are the same kind of thing. "Man", for example, is not the name of an individual but picks out an individual *qua* what he is. Unless Copernicus and Kepler share the same nature, they have nothing in common, but rather there would be only this and that nature, Copernicus' and Kepler's. The same nature, however, receives existence in this and that individual; they are two instances of this nature. As they are the same in respect of their human nature but differ in their existence, that by which they are human and that by which they are this and that human being differs. Scotus goes from essence; the distinction of things for him lies in the "thisness" of every individual's essence. But Aquinas starts with the existence of things: for instance, Copernicus and Kepler were distinct in their existence.

There is a real difference between essence and existence, because things which share the same form do not share the same existence. The only exception is God. As God is identical with His essence and with His existence, His essence is identical with His existence. The reason for this is that everything that begins to exist receives its existence from another. Nothing is the cause of itself, otherwise it would have to exist before itself in order to be able to cause its existence. So nothing can come into existence without something already existing. For a sheep to come into existence, sheep must exist before it, which have been brought into existence before it by other sheep before them and so on. Whatever receives its existence shares in existence, because it receives it from another. But in one thing receiving existence from another, we must eventually come back to something that has not received its existence from another but simply *is*.

What exists, but has not received its existence, *is* its existence. As this being does not receive its existence, neither is its essence *given* existence; its essence simply exists. It also *is* its essence, because it does not share in it by receiving it from another. If its essence received existence, this would be from another and it would be caused. But we have just admitted that, in one thing causing the existence of another, we must go back to something whose existence is not caused by another, or else there would be a question of what caused that, and so on.

This gives us three ways in all, in which things can have their essence and existence. In God, neither essence nor existence is received; He is His essence and is His existence, and He is utterly simple. In immaterial substances, like angels, their essence is not received in anything, for they have no matter. They are their essence, because an angel is just its form, being immaterial. But an angel receives its existence, because it is created; so its essence is given existence. Essence and existence are not identical in angels, as they are in God, because an angel is its essence but not its existence, which it receives from its Creator. Thus an angel is simple in that it is its form and essence; but there is a composition of essence and existence, because its essence receives existence. In material things, however, there is composition both of matter and form and of essence and existence. A material thing is not just its form as an angel is, for it also consists of matter; so there is composition of form and matter in material things as well as of essence and existence. An angel is simple in one way, a material thing is complex in both ways. Thus we have these three ways of existing.

	Essence	Existence
God	Not received	Not received
Immaterial substances	Not received in anything	Received
Material substances	Received in matter	Received

Whatever is not received in anything and does not receive its existence from another is not limited by anything else; therefore it is infinite. Immaterial beings are limited to a particular nature. In material things, form is limited by matter.

These are all the actualities of being: that is, this threefold division covers all beings which actually exist. As everything that receives its existence goes back to something that is its existence, metaphysics leads to "theology", which Aristotle calls the most noble of the sciences, because asking about what brings things into existence in the world takes us back to the cause of all existence. Thus existence leads us on to the topic of causes.

Chapter Six

CAUSES

Human beings naturally want to know, so they ask questions. Scientists ask questions of nature itself. The answer to the question, "Why is it like that?", "Why did it do that?", "Why did it happen?", is often "Because..." To say "The lady died of arsenic", is to state the *cause* of her death. Aristotle defines the wise person as one who seeks the causes of things. Thus, the wise person will want to know the highest cause, the cause of all things. To say that something has a cause is to say it has an explanation. To give an explanation of some event in nature or the world is to give an *account* of it. The Greeks used the same word for an account as they did for a word, *logos. Logos,* as we have already seen, meant a reason as well as a word. To give an account of some event or behaviour is to give a *reason* for it. Thus, a world in which things happen for reasons and have causes is a *rational* world. If, as far as we could see, there were no reason why things happen and are as we find them, the world would seem to be an irrational one to us.

A world with reason comes from a Mind; matter by itself does not have reason. The alternatives are either to say that the world is due to chance or that it is determined. The order we find in the universe is not due to chance. Laws of nature do not come from chance, for they are general rules of the way nature behaves. To be determined is to have a way of acting imposed *on* one. This is from outside, by something or someone else. So we come back to the fact that the world contains reason, because it comes from Mind or the Logos. To discover causes is to think that there is some reason and, consequently, meaning in the world. The discovery of laws of nature, which may be regarded as the greatest achievement of scientists, rests on the assumption that events in nature have causes, which we can find out and know.

What we often first notice, however, is not causes but *effects*, whose cause we then seek. We discover causes from effects. An effect is something produced by a cause. There is no effect without a cause; effects derive from causes. We may then define a cause as something that produces an effect. This implies action, for nothing can be a cause unless it *acts*. It was for this reason that Plato's Forms could not be causes, for he thought that they were unchanging and immobile. Change is an effect of activity, and activity is produced by causes. A cause today almost invariably means an *efficient* cause, which is an agent that initiates some change by acting, as acid changes copper by corroding it, that is by eating into it. The modern idea of cause, however, is a limited one, for there used to be *four* kinds of cause recognized. Aristotle remarks that material things are made *out of* something (their matter), *into* something (by their form), *by* something (an agent), *for* something (a purpose or end). The end of the eye, for example, is to see. This gives us the following kinds of cause.[1]

FOUR KINDS OF CAUSE

The *Material Cause* of a box is wood, of a candle is wax, and of brass is copper and zinc. This is what a thing is made *out of.*

The *Formal Cause* is what makes matter *into* the kind of thing it is, because it is the form it receives which is responsible for this. Marble is made into a statue by being cut with a certain form. Wood with one form is turned into a table, with another form into a boat.

The *Efficient Cause* is the origin of change, because it is the agent that acts. The word "agent" comes from the Latin *agere*, to act. Thus, it initiates the change and produces the effect; hence *efficient* cause. The efficient cause of a statue is a sculptor, of corrosion is acid or salt.

The *Final Cause* of something is what it is *for.* "Final" comes from *finis*, the Latin for "end", and so "purpose". A corkscrew is for drawing corks out of bottles, and the Arc de Triomphe was built to commemorate Napoleon's victories. The final cause is the reason for acting: the English went to war to protect their commercial interests, and the Dutch built dykes to prevent floods and irrigate or drain fields.

We can give some further examples of these different kinds of cause. The material cause of glass is sand, lime and soda, which is fused by the action of a furnace heating them. The efficient cause of a pot is a potter; the potter's wheel is an *instrumental* cause of a pot. An instrumental cause is used by the efficient cause. The final cause of a pot may be to hold flowers. A final cause of trees is to provide shade.

---

[1] Aristotle, *Physics* II c.3.

Modern science has rather forgotten about final causes. Where Aristotle looked for purpose in nature, modern science has looked for laws; science has been more interested in *how* than *why* things work. Some natural scientists even deny the existence of purpose in nature, although it is evident that a great many things in nature have been designed for a purpose or *function*. Camels have humps to carry enough water across the desert, elephants trunks to drink without having to get down on to their knees every time.

To explain the structure and working of things by their purpose, what they are *for*, is to give them a *teleological* explanation (from the Greek *telos*, an end or goal). It has been common in the past century to deny teleology in nature, and to say that plants and animals have evolved by chance mutations. For things to happen by chance is the contrary of them happening for a reason. Things that happen by chance may happen in any way, but this is not what we often observe in nature, which acts in set ways. It is hard to deny that the design of the parts and organs of plants and animals have a purpose or function — for instance of the iris for letting in and shutting out light in the eye, and the curves of bones to bear stresses.

To see that things have a purpose is to see that they come from a mind, for purpose does not come from chance. Nor does matter by itself act for a purpose, because it cannot *conceive* an end for which to act. Purpose then comes from a mind. So when things in nature without mind act for a purpose and end, they do it because they have been given their end, and been made to act in this way by some mind. Aristotle remarks that the final cause often comes first in the sequence of action. For example, the beginning of a mason cutting a tombstone is that someone wants a memorial *for* a grave. To design an aeroplane, the designer first has to decide what the aeroplane is for: to carry ninety or two hundred passengers, say, inside Europe or across the Atlantic. The purpose determines the design. Although the final cause is the last in the order of the four kinds of cause, as the end that something is directed to, it precedes the action of a voluntary agent, because we do not make anything without first having an idea of what we want to make, and what we intend to make is for a purpose. Thus *thought* is a cause of action. To act for a purpose is to act for a *reason*.

In the reproduction and growth of living things, *the final and formal cause coincide*. The end of an acorn is to turn into an oak tree. It turns into something with the same form as produced it, namely an oak tree, because of its own form. Without this an acorn would not grow into something with the same form as produced it. An acorn has a definite end, because it only turns into an oak tree and not into any other kind of tree. Thus the final and formal causes of living things coincide, because they reach their end by their form. A sculptor attains his end of producing a statue by a form he conceives in his mind; the form of a statue is different from the form of the agent who produces it by art, but the form of an oak tree is the same as what produces it by *nature*.

NATURAL AND VOLUNTARY CAUSES

Aristotle says that everything that changes: first, *is* something; second, changes *into* something; and third, is changed *by* something.[2] It is matter, is changed into something by assuming another form and is changed by something that moves it. These three correspond to the material, formal and efficient causes. Flour, for example, is changed into bread

---

[2] *Metaphysics* XII c.3 1069b36.

through the action of a baker and an oven or fire. But flour does not change by itself or its own power into bread. So Aristotle says that things are brought into existence in one of three ways: either by nature or by art or by luck, that is chance. Things often happen by luck or chance when some defect or fault *prevents* things from working in their usual way.

Things either come into existence through an *external* or *internal* agent. When the source of movement comes from outside, it is an external agent, for example the change in shape of a block of marble by a sculptor. When the principle of movement and change springs from within something that moves or changes, the cause is an internal agent. There are two kinds of internal agent: *nature* and *free will*. Bread is made by the art of baking or cooking, but the wheat from which the flour is made is produced by nature. Horses too are produced by nature; they are not made by art. Although all living things are produced by external agents, in that they come from another plant or animal, the generating agents only bring together the male and female elements necessary for reproduction; but once the elements have fused, a new unit of life begins to grow and develop by its *own* power. So growth is caused by an internal agent, which is the body that nourishes itself.

Things grow according to their nature; they cannot alter their nature and grow into another kind of thing from the one that produced them, so a beech nut will not grow into a holly tree or an elm produce the leaves of a sycamore tree. Trees grow by nature, but beds made from trees are not produced by nature. Pine trees produce pine trees, but pine beds do not produce pine beds, for beds are made by the *art* of carpentry when wood is given the form of a bed by an external agent. An external agent gives matter another form than its own; when living things produce something with the same form as themselves they *reproduce* themselves. Swallows reproduce themselves by nature but build nests by art.

Medicine is a cause of health when it is applied to patients; engineering is a cause of bridges when its principles are applied to putting together the parts of a bridge, its stones or metal girders. Medicine and engineering are classed by Aristotle as arts, for they are based on principles discovered by experience as well as science; these sciences are *practical* as well as theoretical.

The other internal agent besides nature is *will*, which springs from within the agent and is a cause of motion. Aristotle names several internal sources of motion. First there is the soul, because it is by the powers of their soul that living things grow, have sensation and move. Without its principle of life, the soul, a living thing has no power to do any of these things. Next, reason and desire are causes of motion. Reason thinks up the ends for which we act; desire of something good moves us towards the thing we apprehend as good and therefore desirable. Animals have desire but they do not have free will in the proper sense; free will goes with reason and *deliberating* about which course of action to take. Free action goes with acting for an end or purpose; animals do not choose ends, as we do, since conceiving an end involves reason.

Cardinal John Henry Newman (1801-1890) even thought that will is the first experience we have of causes: "We have no experience of any cause but Will."[3] We do not see that bodies attract one another by gravity, he says; it is therefore an idea. But I know that I am the cause of making a sound when I touch the keys of a piano or open my mouth and sing. I do these things because I *will* to do them. The first way I know

---

[3] *An Essay in Aid of a Grammar of Assent* (1870; Longman, Green; 1947); p. 55. See generally *Grammar of Assent* Part I c. IV 1, 5-6, on causation (pp. 51-56).

about causes, then, is by willing my own actions. Causation, for Newman, is the idea of power combined with a purpose or end: I will to play a sonata and to achieve this end I move the keys of a piano. Voluntary action is the model of causation for Newman, as it is also for Aristotle: "Starting, then, from experience, I consider a cause to be an effective will."[4]

Newman then goes on to argue that, if nature acts for ends, it comes from a *voluntary* agent: that is, nature has been made by someone with will, who has given everything its end. For example, the end of an acorn is to turn into an oak tree — it does not turn into anything else; this is its natural end.

Nonetheless, there are contemporary philosophers who deny that we can know the real causes of natural events. The late A.J. Ayer, for example, writes: "In nature one thing just happens after another. Cause and effect have their place only in our imaginative arrangements and extensions of these primary facts."[5] He denies that "after this" ever means "because of this". This is contrary to our experience. A chemist can know the causes of chemical reactions when the same experiment, repeated frequently, produces the same result. And he can also know that the reaction occurs because he has set up the experiment.

KINDS OF CHANGE

There is no change without motion. Nature and will are both sources, or principles, of motion. Motion for us primarily means the actions of things like engines and clocks, but for the ancients its primary meaning was *change*. A change may be regarded as the motion from one state to another. Things only

---

[4] Ibid. p.53.
[5] *The Central Questions of Philosophy* (Penguin, 1973), p.183.

change into something they *can* become: lead cannot become gold, but wood can become coal. Thus, a change is from a *potential* to an actual state. Matter has by nature certain powers and potential: for example, grains of salt and sand cannot by themselves contain water. But sand has the power to be turned into glass, with the addition of lime and soda. Sand is potentially glass and is turned into glass by the action of a glass-blower who, with the chemical action of the ingredients and of fire, is the efficient cause of this change: that is, he initiates the action, which produces glass from sand. Thus the sand's power to become glass is actualized. This is by some action. To take an example from living things, a tulip bulb is a potential tulip; when it is set in the ground, it becomes a tulip with the suitable action of water and sunlight. An acorn is a potential oak tree. Changes are the effects of activity (*kinesis*). Activity is produced by an agent, or efficient cause, which sets in motion the change. Nature may be the cause of change in this sense.

Aristotle lists four kinds of change: first, of *essence*, which is by generation and corruption; second, of *quality*, which is an accidental change; third, of *quantity*, by increase and diminution; and fourth, of *place*, which is what we commonly mean by motion.

The change of essence, which is of what something is as a whole, is the corruption of one thing and the generation of a new thing. Corruption and generation mean going out of and coming into existence. For example, when milk is churned into butter, milk ceases to exist and butter comes into existence where there was milk before. With a change of quality, something still remains the same kind of thing; there is no change of the essence. Whether wax is liquid or solid, it still is wax. Likewise, a change of size by becoming more or less can occur without a change of essence: a baby elephant is as much an elephant as a large one. When a body changes place by moving, there is also a physical change as well as one of position, for energy is used up; but it remains an identical body. Aristotle also notes that a change of quality may be from one contrary to another: for example, matter may change from being clear to opaque, but clear does not become opaque. So there must be something *underlying* the change, which has the potential of existing in either state, as when clay can exist in a molten and then brittle and dense state, when it has been cooled. What underlies the change is the *substrate* which was Aristotle's first meaning of substance.

Aristotle distinguishes between two sorts of change: one he calls change, the other merely *alteration*. A change of essence produces a change in the strict sense: one kind of thing goes out of existence, a new one comes into existence in its place. The other kinds of change he calls alteration. Thus we see that what Aristotle calls "change", in the strict sense, occurs when something begins and ceases to exist. When the same thing remains, it is an alteration; for example, when leaves change their colour, this is an alteration.

Not all change is merely alteration, because things do come into and go out of existence. There is not just alteration, as some of the Presocratic philosophers thought, because they held that the world is one great substance — if the world is just one substance, then all that happens is merely alterations of this one substance. But, as we saw in Chapter Four, every individual thing is a substance, with its own existence. Already existing things alter, but new ones also *come into existence*, for example with the invention of a new dye, which was named after the battle of Magenta in 1859 and had not previously existed. With the generation of a human being or a giraffe, a new individual comes into existence. When flour, water and yeast, are turned into bread, a loaf comes into existence; there is one extra loaf, which is a substance, in the world.

Change corresponds with *substantial* change, and alteration with *accidental* change. When clay is fired in an oven, there is a substantial change as it becomes a pot or dish, for it ceases to have the qualities of clay, which is porous and malleable. When bread is toasted, it is altered in quality from soft to hard. But when bread is sufficiently charred there is a substantial change, as it ceases to be bread and becomes charcoal. Some processes are irreversible, as the Second Law of Thermodynamics states. When clay has been fired it cannot turn back into clay; charcoal cannot be restored to bread. When I mix ink with water, I cannot unscramble the ink from the water. These are changes of clay, bread and ink, when the ink is diluted beyond a certain point. When a forester fells a tree, this is not just an alteration of it, like cutting off a few of its branches; the tree goes out of existence, for its life has been destroyed.

There is alteration when the condition of something's matter changes, as when the stones of a cathedral are worn away by the outside agents of air and rain in weathering them. But cathedrals are brought into existence and begin to exist; they are not just alterations of a city. There is a cause of things coming into and going out of existence. Nothing is the cause of itself existing, for it would have to precede itself, to bring itself into existence. Thus, the First Cause of all is simply uncaused. The existence of the cause is *prior* to the effect; if effects preceded causes, we could no longer distinguish between causes and effects. An effect can, of course, be simultaneous with its cause, like the effect of gravity, which acts instantaneously. But the source of gravity already exists. An effect often appears to be simultaneous with its cause, since the effect is produced by removing something which *prevents* the cause from operating. For example, when I light up the room by moving a switch, I remove the disconnection of wires, which prevents the electrical current from reaching the light bulb; but the current that causes the bulb to glow already exists in the wire from the mains. Similarly, lighting up a room is simultaneous with drawing the curtains in the morning, but the sun is shining before what prevents it shining into the room is drawn aside.

Everything that begins to exist has a cause, for nothing is the cause of itself. But not everything that is caused is necessary. Houses and horses have causes but they do not necessarily exist. To be caused is not the same as to be determined. If everything were necessary, there would be no such thing as bringing things into existence by free will. Thus things and events are either necessary or *contingent*. If the world itself has no cause, it is either due to chance or necessity. It is not due to chance, because there is purpose in nature, which cannot be explained by chance. It hardly seems to be by chance that all nine planets revolve round the sun in the same direction and, with the exception of Uranus, on almost the same plane. Nor does the world exist by necessity, because not all nature is necessitated. The world is not necessary, because not all its parts are necessary. So it is due to some third way in between these two: *intention*. Intention comes between chance and necessity, because it is for an end, which is contrary to chance, yet it is not determined but willed. Nature "tends" to act in certain ways, as we recognise when acid always corrodes and heavy bodies fall to the earth from the air, because it is intended to act in those ways. But only *minds* intend things. Thus the world does not exist by necessity but comes from a will; its existence is contingent. Contingent things may or may not exist; they do not have to exist but are *possible*.

NECESSITY AND POSSIBILITY

Things and events are either necessary, possible or impossible. Impossible (cannot possibly be) is the opposite of necessary, which cannot *not* be. Possible things stand between existing and not existing until either their possibility is made actual or irreversibly cut off at some point, when they become impossible. Before the last train left Russia in the revolution of 1917, it was still possible to escape; after it had left, it was impossible to escape. Thus:

Term	Meaning
Necessary	Cannot not be; it is determined in *one* way.
Possible	Can go either way; it can be and can *not* be; it does not have to be and may never be.
Impossible	Cannot be; there is *no* way it can be.

Possible is "A or not A"; necessary is not "not A"; impossible is not "A or not A" ("A or not A" is possibly A). Impossible is not "possibly A"; necessary is not "possibly not A".

A cause may be *necessary* in two ways — either by always producing a certain effect, or by being required for a certain effect, even if it is not enough by itself to produce this effect. In the first way, cause A is *always* followed by effect B (if A, then B); you never get A without B (for instance, lightning without thunder). In the second way, cause A is needed to obtain effect B; you cannot have B without A. For example, there is no flood without heavy rain, but a flood does not always follow heavy rain.

But a necessary cause may not be a *sufficient* cause; other causes as well may be needed to obtain or cause the effect. In this case, although cause A is necessary for effect B, B does not always follow A, and you can have A without B if A is not sufficient for producing B. Plants will not grow and produce flowers without sunlight, but sunlight, though a necessary cause, is not a sufficient one by itself, because plants also need water to grow. A saw is necessary for cutting wood but it is not a sufficient cause unless its teeth have been sharpened and a carpenter applies it to some wood.

On the other hand, a sufficient cause may not be necessary; just because it is enough by itself to cause something, it may not itself be necessary, or necessarily act. A severe frost will necessarily kill vines, but a severe frost in spring may be due to a co-incidence of meteorological causes, which do not necessarily come together. The co-incidence of the causes may be due to chance. To take an example of Aristotle's, a coat will necessarily be cut up or wear out; coats do not last for ever and it is necessary that it cease to exist one way or the other. But this does not mean that whichever comes to pass, getting cut up or wearing out, necessarily happens. It may even be by chance that it gets cut up. Neither cause of the end of the coat is necessary in itself, although it is necessary that one of these two be the cause of its end.

If things are not necessary, they are *contingent*; they may or may not happen — they are, but could have been otherwise. Many events in the world are *accidental*. Accidents are due to a coincidence of causes, like the collision of two vehicles or two ships when their separate paths intersect at the same time. The crossing of the causes is not necessary but accidental.

For example, to take another famous case from antiquity, a man goes out to a field and digs to plant a tree, and while digging he discovers treasure buried in the field. He did not dig in order to look for treasure; he finds it by chance, because it was not his intention in digging. It may be a chance that he chose that corner of the field for planting his tree; it may also have been a chance that the treasure was deposited there, perhaps by force of unforeseen circumstances when its bearers were intending to take it further. Digging is a necessary cause of his finding treasure, because he would not have found it without digging, yet finding the treasure was accidental, because it was not necessary for him to plant a tree or dig in that part of the field.

Scientists make discoveries by chance, because they happen to leave something in the way of something else without knowing it will have the effect which they then notice. Röntgen, for example, discovered X-rays by accident as the cause of the fluorescence on a screen of barium, which happened to be near to a tube in which he was conducting some experiments with gases and electricity.

Events that happen for no purpose or reason happen by *chance*. Two friends separately set out for two particular shops in the town centre and, on their way, meet in the market square. They meet by chance, because each did not set out with the intention of meeting the other; it is by chance that they cross paths, although it is not by chance that they set out for the town centre. A man crossing the desert will necessarily seek a well when he becomes thirsty, but be murdered by chance, if brigands reach the well at the same time on their way from, say, Cairo to Khartoum, for a quite different purpose, to sell their merchandise.

But not everything can be due to chance, for chance *presupposes* causation. Chance is accidental, but nothing can be accidental without being accidental *to* something. Chance also presupposes causes, because those who deny causes require a way of distinguishing "chance" from "not chance".[6] Someone

---

[6] Aristotle, *Physics* II c. 8.

who asserts that everything happened by chance is unable to provide a reason for his claim, since he must admit that his thought itself comes by chance. So, if everything is due to chance, one cannot uphold or prove the view that everything is due to chance on rational grounds. But there would not be the regularity we observe in nature if everything were due to chance.

A nice example of the chance meeting of causes provides the plot of Thornton Wilder's long short story *The Bridge of San Luis Rey*. Was it just a chance that those five people were on the bridge together when it snapped in 1714, or was there some explanation of their crossing it at the same time? What looks like a random collection of people on the bridge at the time of its collapse turns out to have a thread running through the lives of all of them, going back to one person in Lima, who directs the course of each one. It is a parable of providence, which is God's directing of the world. What seems to be merely a coincidence may have some reason or cause. On the other hand, what seems to be necessary because inevitable, may not be so, as G.K. Chesterton points out in one of his Father Brown stories, *The Doom of the Darnaways*. Although a member of the family is murdered in every generation, no one is *doomed* to be murdered, because murder is an act of free will, so is not necessitated.

Some things, however, do come about by chance. A good instance of this is the slaying of King Ahab in battle. He was mortally wounded by an arrow shot at random. The archer who shot the arrow cannot have intended to hit the king, because Ahab entered the battle disguised.[7] The archer may not have aimed at any one, but just shot an arrow into the air.

---

[7] I Kings 22:34.

Effects may be probable, though the cause is not probable. If someone strays on to a beach he will probably tread on one of the mines still buried on that beach, but it is not likely that anyone will go onto that beach if there are signs warning of the danger.

Actions may have causes but not a reason. I may spill coffee in a train because it unexpectedly sways. Although I do not spill my coffee for a reason, there is a cause of my spilling it — the sudden movement of the train. In this case my action is involuntary.

We also distinguish between *grounds* and *motives* of an action. Motives are emotions like gratitude, fear, envy or anger. One may be moved to act out of pity. Having grounds is having reasons for acting. Reasons are steps thought out to bring about an end; they are the result of *deliberation*. One may commit murder out of anger without reasoning about it, or as the deliberate means of robbing the victim. In the first case, one has a motive, in the second an *intention*. But this does not mean that the first is not voluntary; the murderer still *chooses* to kill out of anger.

Motives may explain actions, but they do not *necessarily* cause them; *will* is involved, because it is possible to be angry and not to commit murder. Motives are like feelings. A motive is a cause, but it may also be against reason, as with fear when the object of one's fear does not really exist. But a motive may also be a *reason* for acting: for example, doing a favour in return out of gratitude for having received help in the past.

HUME ON CAUSES

We have seen that everything that begins to exist, or comes into existence, has a cause but does not necessarily exist. Therefore not all causes are necessary. This was denied by David Hume (1711-1776), who held that the only causes are necessary causes, but this holds precisely in the sense that we only know something is a cause if it always happens that way. As cause and effect are distinct, he says that the one can be imagined without the other and therefore that there is no necessary connection between them. Thus, we cannot know causes. Again, the key to understanding Hume on causes is his principle that all ideas are derived from impressions. We only get the idea of cause, he says, from observing the *constant conjunction* of things, for example of clouds and rain.[8] But we do not know that one thing causes another, because we only have impressions of the two objects and not of their connection. As he admits that this is the most violent paradox of his thought, namely that the sight of two things together does not produce the idea of their connection, perhaps he was not quite easy about it.

Hume denies that we can know real causes for three reasons. First, the only way we could tell that one thing causes another is if A always goes with B; if B does not always follow A, we cannot conclude that A is the cause of B. Thus Hume thought that all causes must be necessary.[9] But as we cannot infer the cause from the effect unless the connection is necessary (that is, it cannot be otherwise), we cannot know the real causes of things, and cause is just an idea (or "internal impression" as he calls it) of the mind. In Hume's view, we do

---

[8] *A Treatise of Human Nature* I iii 6.
[9] Ibid. I iii 14.

not know the real connection, but only make one in our minds.

Second, Hume says, producing an effect implies that the cause has the *power* to do this. But as we only have impressions of sensible qualities, and power is not a sensible quality, we have no impression of power, and power is just an idea. According to Hume, we do not see that something has the power to do something — for example, a wave to knock me down. Since we have no idea that is not derived from an impression, Hume denies that reason alone can ever give rise to a new idea. Against this, one may ask from what impression we get the idea of infinity, yet the use of this idea in mathematics is quite acceptable. Hume limits the power of the mind to go beyond observation in reasoning about what is perceived by the senses. The idea of cause for him is no more than that of constant conjunction, but he does not allow that we can penetrate to the *reason* for the conjunction. So nothing new can be discovered, since ideas do not add anything to impressions. They do not add anything, because they are just copies of impressions. As reasoning *presupposes* ideas, Hume says that it is unable to produce new ones.

His third reason is that we need to observe more than one instance of the conjunction of two things to know that one is the cause of the other. But we only have impressions of single instances, none of which is by itself sufficient to give us the idea of cause and effect. Since we never arrive at the idea of cause and effect from any one instance, we have no impression of them from which we could derive the idea of them.[10] The history of science refutes Hume here, since a single observation has sometimes been enough for a scientist

---

[10] Ibid. I iii 14.

to see a law, which has then been confirmed by further observation and experiment.

Hume's idea of cause and effect is entirely founded on past experience, not on any insight that the world is a rational one, in which there is an ordered and regular connection of things that we can know. Hume does not consider that things can be known *generally*, because some things always have certain effects or are always found to come from particular causes. The mind is not led by reason to new discoveries and insights according to Hume, because he limits its working to the association of ideas. He makes the idea of cause depend on thought rather than thought on causes. If thought is caused by the perception of external things, why may there not be causes of things and events as well as of our thoughts? Yet Hume did think that our perceptions and ideas are caused.

With a knowledge of causes, I am able to make things happen as I expect; this should be impossible, according to Hume, if we are unable to know real causes. A natural scientist designs an experiment using the knowledge he already has of what causes what. This knowledge is the common possession of scientists. Moreover, the effect of medicaments, including their side-effects, are known by pharmacists and doctors; only on the basis of this knowledge are they prescribed. I *know* that sunlight causes plants to flower, if they do not produce flowers in a dark room but do so in a bright one.

Hume argued that we do not know that one thing causes another, but only *infer* the existence of one thing from another by experience.[11] Nothing implies the existence of something else for Hume, because if it did, it would have to be that way and could not be otherwise. The way to get out of this circular argument is to recognise that something is not

---

[11] Ibid. I iii 14.

necessary just because it is caused; many things are caused which might not have existed, for example works of art produced by artists.

Hume goes so far as to say that, because the ideas of cause and effect are distinct, we can conceive any object not to have a cause.[12] If it does not have a cause, it is not an effect. Yet we know that certain things always are effects: for example, clothes are made from wool which is produced by sheep that come from sheep before them, and so on. We have seen that everything that has a beginning of existence has a cause of its existence, but for Hume, a bag of wool or a coat could suddenly appear in a shop without a cause. This is certainly not anything that we know from experience, although Hume says that we derive all our ideas from experience.

But how does Hume know that we have no impression of cause unless he already has the idea of cause? To deny that we can have the idea of cause from impressions, he must first assume the very idea he denies that we can derive from them. Or how can he insist that ideas be derived from impressions when he shows that he already has the idea of cause? Must not the idea, then, come from reason, which Hume says is unable to produce any new idea?

Immanuel Kant (1724-1804), rescues the idea of cause by saying that it is justified because it alone makes the phenomena of the world intelligible. He differs from Hume in his approach to the idea, for Hume makes it an induction *from* experience, but Kant makes it a *presupposition* for having experience. In Kant's view, *we* make the world intelligible by our ideas, rather than discover the intelligibility of the world. Order is not so much anything we find in the world as it is *imposed* by us on the phenomena. If the order is imposed by us,

---

[12] Ibid. I ii 6.

it is remarkable that natural scientists can agree about the order and do not impose various ways of seeing the world. There would not be one natural science shared by scientists all over the world unless they could agree about an objective order in nature. That natural science is universal witnesses to the existence of this order in nature itself, not just in our minds. Kant weakens the idea of cause, because it is little more than the succession of things for him; something is an effect because it comes after something else. He requires the idea to explain phenomena.

Twentieth century physics has shown that the world is much less determined than it was thought to be in the eighteenth and nineteenth centuries. Since atomic physics shows that the movement of particles is indeterminate, the very idea of causation has come into question. Now one no longer speaks of laws of nature, but of patterns of events and statistical probabilities, without being able to predict what particles will do in any one instance — only what they on average do in so many out of, say, a hundred instances. Yet it is still possible to predict eclipses and the return of comets accurately. Natural science would never have been pursued unless men had thought that causes exist, and it would not exist unless it were possible to discover causes.

Causes, however, are not to be confused with laws of nature, which "are not the causes but the representations of order".[13] Laws of nature, however, require a separate chapter.

---

[13] E. Whittacker, *Space and Spirit* (Nelson, 1947), p. 84.

Chapter Seven

LAWS OF NATURE

The laws of nature are not causes but tell us *how* things happen. They tell us about the order of the universe: things do not just move in any way or merely at random but follow certain rules or laws. In a similar way, a game of chess can only proceed according to the rules of chess; the rules do not tell us which moves will be made, but how the pieces may be moved — knights may only move in a certain way, bishops and rooks in other ways. Unless the players obey the rules, the game quickly ends in chaos. The laws of nature state *forms* of regular ways of acting and reacting, just as the rules of chess give us the forms of the movements of knights and bishops, rectangular and diagonal.

Although laws of nature are not causes but tell us how causes act and move, they have been discovered by scientists seeking to know the causes of nature: for example, why do the planets revolve round the sun in ellipses? Therefore, knowledge of laws of nature means that we can know real causes. Conversely, we would not know the causes of many things in nature unless they acted according to certain laws, for without these anything or nothing might account for their movement. But the *uniform* way we observe things to act in nature witnesses to the existence of laws in nature.

The discoveries of atomic physics in this century about the *unpredictable* ways in which particles move has somewhat deflected our attention from the open book of nature on the larger scale and especially from the orderly movements of the heavenly bodies which impressed the ancients. It should be remarked that it is not certain that the very conditions of the apparatus used in experiments of physics do not influence the behaviour of particles. Nonetheless, the discoveries of atomic physics in this century have shaken belief in laws of nature.

There are, then, two main questions about the laws of nature. First, are there any laws of nature or is there just a succession of events, which we can describe but not explain? A law is an explanation of the phenomena. And secondly, are the laws of nature discoveries of what really exists in nature or are they products of our thought, imposed by the mind on nature? In other words, are they inventions of the mind and mere hypotheses, not discoveries about nature?

Wittgenstein wrote early in his life that it is only an *hypothesis* that the sun will rise tomorrow.[1] But at the end of his life, one of his arguments for knowing at least some things with *certainty* was that, if some things failed to happen, this would overturn our view of the universe and hence the basis for rational discussion.[2] Among these things, we may include the rising of the sun tomorrow. It is not a law in itself that the sun will rise tomorrow, but if it does not rise one morning, this will be because certain laws, those of gravitation, have been suspended or gone awry.

---

[1] *Tractatus* 6. 36311.
[2] *On Certainty* 114, 160, 209, 342.

Hume, too, argued that we cannot know causes unless we know that it will *always* be so, and that we do not know that the sun will rise tomorrow, in that it is possible that it will not. Even though we cannot know that the sun will not fail to rise on some occasion in the future, if, or rather *as*, it has always risen in the past, this is quite enough for us to form a law. Where Hume says that, although the sun has always risen in the past, there is no reason why it may not tomorrow, Cardinal Newman asks instead: "If it has happened once, why should it not happen twice? Nay, rather what is to hinder it?"[3] And anyway, when something fails to happen out of the ordinary, we naturally look for a *cause* of it not happening on this occasion.

Stephen Toulmin says that the laws of nature are not just hypotheses.[4] He points out that the use of several fundamental terms of science, such as mass, force, momentum, inertia and refraction, *presuppose* laws of nature, because these terms first received their accepted meaning in the statement of certain laws. If a law is only an hypothesis, the terms used in it have no precise meaning. So, if you are going to question whether laws of nature really exist, you also question the foundation of the basic terms with which scienctific discussion is conducted. But before we discuss laws of nature any further, it will be useful to have in our view a few examples of what we are talking about. Let us therefore briefly state three scientific laws which can serve as examples:

Galileo's law about the acceleration of falling bodies — the distance covered is proportional to the square of the time taken, so that a body reaches four times the distance covered in the first unit of time after two units of time, and nine times the distance after three units of time and so on.

---

[3] *A Grammar of Assent* I iv 1, 6, p.55.
[4] *The Philosophy of Science* (Hutchinson, 1953), p. 72.

Newton's Third Law — every action is opposed by an equal and opposite reaction. A body loses whatever motion it communicates to another. Every body attracts another with a force proportional to its mass, hence all bodies fall at the same speed, because a heavier body, which might be expected to fall faster than a light one, also opposes the attraction of the earth's gravity with a greater resistance of its own inertial mass than a lighter one does.

Boyle's Law — the pressure of gas, at a given temperature, varies inversely to the increase or decrease of its volume; so the same amount of gas in half the volume has twice the pressure.

The reasons for holding that there are laws of nature can be divided into four sorts: that we have *general* knowledge; that they apply throughout the universe; that the world is rational; and that we take them into account when we exercise our free will.

First, then, we have *general* knowledge, for example, of the refraction of light in mirrors and water. We do not just have knowledge of isolated and contingent events in nature. It is not contingent whether, on a given occasion a flame needs oxygen to burn; such a flame always does so. The laws of nature do not just apply in some instances; they are general. We are able to predict events like eclipses, the tides and phases of the moon, because the laws of nature continue to hold.

Second, the laws of nature are also *universal*: that is, they are known to operate beyond our solar system and, we may suppose, throughout the universe. For example, the speed at which light travels is constant; the Doppler effect enables us to know whether stars are approaching or receding. Hertz's lines in the spectrum show that stars consist of the same chemical elements as are found on the earth and that these elements react in the same way.

Similarly, gravitation also works beyond this solar system, as binary stars demonstrate. The planet Neptune was discovered, in 1846, on the basis of the known law of gravitation as the explanation of irregularities observed in the orbit of Uranus. Using this law, two astronomers, Adams and Leverrier, were able, in the previous year, to predict where a new planet would be found. It was by assuming that the same law of gravity held for Jupiter that Roemer was able to account for the discrepancy in time of the reappearance of the moons of Jupiter as it was nearer to or further from the earth, by supposing that light takes time to travel. In 1690, he noticed that there was a delay in the expected reappearance of the moons from the other side of Jupiter when it was further from the earth.

Third, we can argue that the world is *rational*, because it has been possible to predict things solely on the basis of mathematics, which is logical. For example, the bending of rays of light round the sun, according to Einstein's General Theory of Relativity, was confirmed by observation of the eclipse of the sun in 1919. A single observation can be enough to lead to the discovery of a law, which is then confirmed by subsequent testing. The inverse square law of the force of gravity was a mathematical intuition of Newton's, not anything that he had repeatedly observed.

Further, we can ask whether it is likely that rational beings would exist in an irrational universe? Those who suppose that the universe does not come from a mind will also argue that human beings have arisen from matter by evolution. But why should beings with reason arise in a world not made with reason?

The rationality of the world is the basis of scientific experiments which are conducted by using knowledge of the laws of nature. They are designed with the expectation that certain things and chemicals behave in particular ways. If you deny that there are laws of nature, the results of experiments cannot be used to establish anything general. But many established facts, for example about crystals, are the result of careful experiment. Knowledge of laws of nature is *presupposed* in the pursuit of natural science.

Natural science assumes that the same effects have the same causes. If laws of nature do not exist, things may behave in any way. We could not then speak of them acting according to their *nature*. It is because things regularly act in certain ways that we can tell what is their nature. For example, it is the nature of copper to dissolve in sulphuric acid; it does not just do this sometimes and not at others.

When scientists try to work out what must have happened in the first three seconds of the universe, they can only do this on the basis of the existing laws of nature. In calculating how the universe expanded to reach its present state, they *assume* laws of nature. If an exception occurs, which disproves a law, scientists straightaway look for the *cause* of the exception and try to find a new law, which includes the exception.

Things as different as birds and aeroplanes obey the same laws of aerodynamics. The surface area of an aeroplane's wings is extended when it comes in to land, just as a bird spreads its wings when it is about to alight on the ground or water. We could not design aeroplanes to fly or now build bridges, arches and towers, without knowing the laws of nature about gravity and thrust and stress.

The science of medicine, which studies diseases and seeks their cures, assumes that diseases are not inexplicable but have causes. The discoveries of chemistry also apply to the way that the bodies of animals work; chemistry and biochemistry agree with one another.

The physical universe would be unintelligible to us if we could not find the reasons for things happening in nature. We only know reasons and causes if things generally act in a certain way. When things generally act in set ways, we are able to discern laws in nature.

Fourth, we note that we also assume these laws in making free choices: for example, when we throw things, we judge the force to use, knowing that bodies travel in a parabola through the air because of gravity. Free will fits into a world governed by laws of nature; we take account of these laws in many of our everyday actions.

The laws of nature, however, do not say how things must be; there is no logical necessity about them. A world with different laws of nature could have been created.[5] But they do say how things are in the existing universe. Nor do the laws of nature explain everything: they explain how the planets revolve around the sun but do not tell us *why* there are nine planets or why there is a solar system.[6]

The Nobel prize-winner Richard Feymann admitted that the fundamental laws of nature are not explained by any natural agent. There are laws of nature, but it is not a law of nature that there are laws of nature. Laws of nature do not come into existence by chance; if it were by chance that the universe exists in its present state, the laws might change at any moment. But scientists assume that some things in nature are *constant*. Laws have to be thought up; they come from a *mind*. There would be no laws if the world were merely the result of chance movements of matter.

The laws of nature reflect the order of the universe; and order, Cardinal Newman says, implies a purpose. Order at least means that things are not at variance one with another, or

---

[5] L. Wittgenstein, *Tractatus* 6. 371.
[6] Ibid., 6.32.

in conflict because they are straining in different directions. Order implies a purpose because what gives things order is that they have the same direction.[7] Purpose, as we have seen, comes from a mind. Order, too, implies a mind giving everything its end, otherwise things would have any and contrary directions. The principle of order, Newman says, is a proof of intelligence.

Max Planck, the father of Quantum theory, said: "The more general a law of nature is, the *simpler* is its form." (My emphasis.) Feymann, too, noted that simplicity is a characteristic of nature. This would not be so if nature were just random, for moving at random is taking any path; but simplicity requires economy of movement and design.

Natural science would never have arisen unless it had been thought that we can find the reasons for things happening in nature. In other words, it assumes there is rationality and *logos* in the universe. If it were not possible to show that nature acts according to laws, science would only be able to provide a chronicle of events without any general patterns. If there are no laws, we cannot give a *scientific* account of nature.

Laws of nature presuppose that we can speak of things having natures. Today, however, it is doubted whether things have natures at all. So we next need to examine the idea of nature.

---

[7] *A Grammar of Assent* I iv 1, 6, p.53.

Chapter Eight

NATURES

It is of some practical importance whether there are such things as natures, for we cannot decide who or what is to be counted as a human being, deserving to be treated as one like ourselves, unless we have a concept of human nature. Yet our natural way of speaking indicates that things have natures. For instance, one can find in horticultural shops packets of seeds marked "Mixed flowers". Obviously none of the seeds in the packet is of something called a mixed flower, for every seed is of one or another definite species of flower.

Today, however, it is common to question whether things have natures. This goes back to John Locke (1632-1704), who denied that natures are real and said that they are mere ideas and inventions of the human mind. One of his reasons for denying that natures are real was the case of monsters. Since it is uncertain to which species a monster belongs, he argued that there are no real boundaries in nature. He mentions the case of a prelate, the Abbé Malotru, who was so deformed that he nearly did not pass for a human being at birth.[1] A monster, however, is always a defective instance of some species; it would not be regarded as a monster, unless things have natures and belong to kinds, from which it is an exception. An animal may be a cross between a dog and a wolf, but we are able to say between which two definite species it stands.

Another reason why Locke thought that things do not have definite natures is that it was not possible for chemists in his day to isolate pure examples of the chemical elements.[2] So he used this as an argument that there are no real boundaries in nature and that the distinctions we draw between one species and another are arbitrary divisions of what in nature is one continuous spectrum.

It is, however, no accident that the atomic weights of the elements are proportional to simple whole numbers. Thus, the distinction between natural kinds seems to be clearly marked and to lie in nature itself. This agrees with the fact that each element corresponds with a distinct band of lines in the spectrum, which also appears in the photographs of stars. If Locke had considered that living things only produce offspring with the *same* form as themselves, he might have recognised that plants and animals have definite natures. The cones of cedars of Lebanon do not produce Atlas or deodar cedars; a London plane tree does not produce an oriental plane, and so on.

The key to understanding Locke on natures is his theory of language. Words for Locke are signs of ideas. Ideas, however, are subjective for him, because simple ideas are of sensible qualities, and sensible qualities are the ways that external objects affect us, which can be different in different people. Since everyone has his own ideas, the meaning of

---

[1] *An Essay concerning Human Understanding* III c. 6, 27.
[2] Ibid. III c. 6, 8.

words, too, is subjective; they stand for the ideas of the speaker. By frequent use, words excite in others the ideas for which the speaker uses them. When the speaker excites the same idea in the hearer as he or she has, someone speaks intelligibly. The emperor Augustus, however, said that there was one thing he did not have the power to do: to appoint which idea a sound should stand for or to give words a new meaning.

For Locke, there are two ways of getting our ideas: one is from sensible qualities of external things, the other from reflection on the internal working of the mind. We do not invent simple ideas, for they come from sensible qualities; I cannot, for instance, conceive of a sixth sense.

But abstract ideas are made by the understanding, and natures are abstract ideas according to Locke. Words are general, he says, when we apply them to many things. General names stand for sorts and kinds of things: for example, granite, rose, shell, ivory, deer. But the sorting of plants, animals and minerals is the work of the human understanding for him, not anything already existing in nature. As words stand for our ideas, rather than for things, according to Locke, so the objects of our thought are not things but ideas. Since the names of different natures were signs of ideas for him, it followed that natures were merely ideas and so creations of the human mind.[3] The same does not hold for simple ideas, for these are of sensible qualities and we do not invent these.

If we create natures, or essences, essences did not exist before there was human language, and sea horses, for example, might have existed without the sea horse nature until human beings had a word for them. We do not invent the essences of things that existed before us, for nothing exists

---

[3] Ibid. III c.3, 12.

without a nature, which distinguishes it from everything that does not belong to the same kind.

Mathematicians, however, may be said to invent essences in that they see different figures contained within a figure. For example, a rectangle with sides twice as long as its ends contains a parallelogram and two equal triangles, each of which is one half of the area of the parallelogram, for this oblong consists of two squares.

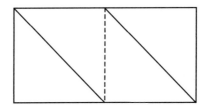

Triangle and parallelogram are kinds of shape; they have essences in that they have definite properties. Elizabeth Anscombe draws the conclusion that the essences of natural things are not creations of the human mind, but of whoever created human nature. She questions the argument that human nature arose of itself from matter, since it is rational. Some, however, think that because bits of matter in computers can perform the operations of intelligent beings, therefore the human mind came about by the movements of bits of matter by itself. But they overlook the fact that computers have been made by human intelligence. So, she concludes, perhaps human nature has also been made by an Intelligence.[4]

Locke held that general ideas are creations of the human mind because he thought that ideas are of features given in

---

[4] *Human Essences* (unpublished paper), International Conference of Philosophers, Brighton, 1988.

sense experience, and concepts are formed by picking out features given in experience. So, he did not think that we could form concepts of *kinds* of things. But Peter Geach shows that Locke's theory of how we form concepts is mistaken, using the example of chromatic colour, which is colour that is not black, white or grey. "Chromatic" and "colour" are two distinct concepts, but I do not get the concept of chromatic colour and, say, purple from distinct features of purple cloth, for it is by one and the same feature that it is purple and chromatically coloured.[5] Nothing is coloured without having a particular colour. The mind, however, goes above sense experience, because colour is a higher, more general concept, as it covers all particular colours.

One way of deciding whether our divisions of things into kinds is arbitrary or lies in nature itself, is to ask yourself whether you could think of another system of colours. Our way of distinguishing colours seems to be grounded in nature, for the colours of the spectrum do not occur in any order, but always with red and violet on the fringes. Wittgenstein asked whether we had a colour system as we had a number system, or if it was an invention of our minds.[6] The system of whole numbers lies in nature, for natural things are wholes, so natural numbers are not just human inventions.

Common nouns, such as swan and ostrich, are the names of sorts for Locke, and sorts are collections of ideas. What marks one sort from another is that it has a different essence. Locke distinguishes between two kinds of essence: real and nominal. The *real* essence of something is its unknown internal constitution, which makes it different from everything of another nature: for example, whatever it is that

---

[5] *Mental Acts* (Routledge & Kegan Paul, 1957), p. 37.
[6] *Zettel* 357.

makes gold different from all other metals. But we do not know what the real essence is, Locke says: it is as remote from the ideas we have of a thing's sensible qualities as the internal mechanism of a clock is from its face. We cannot tell what its mechanism is like from its face. The *nominal* essence is the idea for which the word "gold" stands: a rich yellow, heavy, malleable substance that only dissolves in *aqua regia* (nitric and hydrochloric acid).

Since we do not know the real essences of things, Locke, not surprisingly, thought that nominal essences are collections of ideas: for instance, of shiny, heavy and malleable for gold. Names for Locke, then, signify nominal, not real essences; they signify our ideas rather than things themselves. And the essences for which our names stand are just ideas made by our minds, rather than anything real in nature.

The empiricist philosopher John Stuart Mill (1806-1873), however, thought that our distinction of the kinds of things is grounded in nature. He observed that "man" is the name of a species, but "Christian", "Eskimo", "musician" are not natural distinctions or, therefore, kinds. Mill's way of distinguishing between natural and man-made classes was to ask whether there is a class to which, for example, Socrates but not every human being belongs. If it is a class to which some but not all human beings belong, such as musicians, it is not a distinction of nature. One can be a human being without being an Eskimo, a musician or a philosopher; so these are man-made classes, but human being is a natural kind. Mill also notes that one of the things which distinguishes natural from artificial kinds, like chairs and radios, is that you soon run out of common properties of an artifical kind but keep on discovering more and more common properties of individuals of a natural kind.

Does what all foxes have in common, which makes them one kind, reside in our mind or in nature itself? The reason why we think that they are a distinct species is not just because we see them the same way but because they are alike. We see them as they are in reality. Resemblances between things do not just exist in our minds but also lie in nature. The distinctions of natural kinds of animals, plants and minerals, is not arbitrary or artificial but natural, in Mill's view.[7]

Linnaeus based his system of classifying plants on common features found in nature. Mill said that we could not think of the world as we do unless it had repeated features. Thus it does not just consist of particular individuals, but universals lie *in natura rerum*, in the very nature of things. We have not invented patterns, but discern ones that already exist in nature. Mill pointed out that, even if we grant Locke his view that our ideas of natures are formed from collections of properties, the occurrence of particular groups of properties is still caused; they do not come together without a cause. Thus, the groups of properties which constitute different natures originate in nature, not in our minds. The co-existence of several properties has its cause in nature.

Unless things have natures and particular ways of acting and reacting, we cannot have scientific knowledge. Having a nature means that there is a certain way things act; they do not act in any way. If they did not have their natures, they would act in all manner of unpredictable ways and it would not be possible to establish assured knowledge on the basis of the results of experiments. Science is of its nature general; it does not just tell us what happened in single instances, but its discoveries are valid for all instances of similar conditions. Moreover, it is the existence of natures which secures

---

[7] The System of Logic I vii 4.

permanence and cohesion in a changing universe, so that what was true of water in previous ages is still true of it now. Without the constant properties of the elements and natures, the universe may completely change and lose its coherence. But we suppose that its present order has endured, going back for ages in the past.

When Locke denied that natures are real, he was following in a tradition of philosophers before him. For the roots of his thought, which still is influential today, we turn back to the nominalists, who were so called because they thought, as Locke did, that our general words are mere names.

Chapter Nine

NOMINALISM

In the previous chapter, we saw that our words for natures are general names. There have been three main views about the existence of natures. Plato thought that the Forms or Ideas were the essences of things (for instance, Beauty itself and *the* Horse), and that these essences were the real things, existing on their own. He says that phenomena, meaning things in this world, take the names of the Ideas that they participate in.[1] The second view is that natures are real, but they only exist in individual things, not on their own, as Plato thought. According to this view, our common nouns or names *signify* natures, but *stand for* individuals which have the nature. General names signify natures, because the definition of a word like "fox" or "horse" gives the nature of a fox or horse; but these names refer to individuals with the nature in the way we use the words.[2]

---

[1] Phaedo 102b.
[2] Aquinas, *Summa* I q. 13, 1.

The third view, however, does not think that natures, or essences, have any real existence, but that our names which express natures do not name anything in reality and are thus *only* names. Hence this view is known as *nominalism*, from *nomen*, the Latin for name. *Nomen* also means "noun" in Latin. Nominalism is the doctrine that general words are just names, because they are only ideas of the human mind. Names are either common (for example, duck, fox, peacock, cardamom, bitumen) or proper (Socrates, Kepler, Celestine and Copenhagen). "Copenhagen" itself is the name of a city and of a horse. Names are like the words we write on labels to signify which kind of jam or which colour something is: for example, apricot, orange, magenta. When we use the name "fox", we usually mean an individual animal, but "fox" is not the name of an animal, because it is applied to many animals, to everything that is a fox. Thus "fox" is the name of a *kind* of animal, that is, of something of a particular nature, and we use it for all individuals with that nature.

Two-Term Theory

Nominalism is also known as the "Two-Term Theory", because it treats the subject and predicate alike as two names and holds that the subject and predicate words are names of one and the same thing. Thus "This rose is red" means "the redness of this rose"; "rose" and "red" name the redness of a particular rose.[3] From this we see that nominalists only talk about individual things, the redness of this rose and of that rose; but do not recognise anything common between them in reality, like their redness. For a nominalist, an abstract word

---

[3] For a modern version of this theory, see B. Russell, *Meaning and Truth*, p. 41.

like "redness" or "roundness" or "bitterness" is just a name; it does not name anything in reality, but only an idea in our minds. It is, however, inconsistent to say that "This rose is red" names the redness of this rose, but that "redness" is just an abstract word that does not name anything real.

Nominalists turn the "is" of predication (that is, the copula) into the "is" of identity: instead of "clear" being a predicate in "the fountain is clear", "fountain" and "clear" name one and the same thing, the clarity of the fountain. Peter Geach, however, points out that predicates are not names; rather they are *true or false* of things. He reminds us that names name objects, but we do not predicate objects of things, as we would if predicates were names. A name always names something but, if "duck" were a name in "Jemima is a duck", we could ask which duck is Jemima. But it is pointless to ask which duck is Jemima; rather we are saying something that is true or false of Jemima. So "duck" is not a name but a predicate here, and says that Jemima is something with the duck nature or form.[4]

Likewise, when we say, "Kepler was an astronomer", we do not name an astronomer that Kepler became. If predicates were names, "Kepler was a mathematician" and "Kepler was an astronomer" would stand for two different things, whereas "mathematician" and "astronomer", in this case, are true of one and the same subject. The predicate applies, or does not apply if false, to that which the subject word names. For example, in "St. Michael is an archangel", "archangel" rightly applies to the individual named by the subject word "St. Michael". Moreover, the archangel nature has real existence in St. Michael; the *truth* of this sentence goes with the existence of this nature in reality. Thus truth and reality go together.

---

[4] *Reference and Generality* (Cornell, 1962), p.35.

How is it true to say that someone is an archangel unless we are speaking of something real? But archangel, like fox and horse, names a nature.

Let us now take the sentence "Barbar is an elephant." Is not "elephant" here a name? If "Barbar" and "elephant" were names of the same object, there would be a question of which elephant Barbar is. But we are not asking or saying which elephant; rather "elephant" here is the name of a nature or form. "Barbar" is the name of something with the elephant form. Elephant is used here as predicate.

Frege teaches that general terms, like elephant and planet, are not names but *stand for* forms when used in the position of the predicate (for example, "x is an elephant", "x is a planet"). Likewise, when we say, "Some mammals swim in the sea", "mammals" names individuals, as it is in the position of the subject; but when we say, "Some things that swim in the sea are mammals", we predicate the mammal nature or form of things like whales and seals, which swim in the sea. The word "fish" is similarly used in two different ways in "Fish swim in the sea" and "Whales are not fish". The use of "not" in this second sentence brings out that "fish" here is a predicate that is true or false of the subject "whales".

The above examples show us that predicates are not names and that the Two-Term Theory does not correspond with the natural way we use language. We may now look briefly at one of the chief representatives of the nominalist school, the Franciscan friar William of Ockham (1285-1349).

OCKHAM

Ockham is famous for "Ockham's Razor". His metaphorical razor is meant to eliminate unnecessary "entities". What Ockham said was not "Do not multiply entities more than necessary", as is often thought, but "Do not do with many what can be done with few." This refers to the fact that he wanted to abolish the distinction between essence and existence, since he held that for Socrates to exist is the same as for him to be a man or human, which is his essence. But we may object that the existence of this man is not the same as the existence of that man. So they differ in existence, yet share the same nature, otherwise we could not call them by the same name "man" or "human", which signifies the nature.

Ockham also wanted to cut out abstract words and terms, which arise from our classifying things, because he said that individuals exist, not classes of things. Examples of classifying are "words", "speech" and parts of speech, like "verb", "noun", "tense" and "persons". It would be difficult to do without these words in explaining grammar, which gives us the *logical* structure of thought and language.

Ockham held that, as we only know individual instances of things, so there is nothing universal in reality. Consequently, he thought that we only *intuit* what things are. For example, I see a large animal and intuit that it is a bear, because in reality there is nothing common between bears, but only this and that individual, which we call a "bear". So, with a sentence like "Every bear is an animal", if "animal" does not name anything real that bears have in common, every bear is just this and that animal. But the question remains: what makes anything an animal, if not anything real that they have in common?

As the only things that really exist are individuals for Ockham, it follows that there is no real connection between things, and as we are unable to see any real relation between them, we cannot know that one thing is the *cause* of another, since being a cause implies a relation to its effect. Without real causes we are unable to show by reason that God exists as the cause of the world. For knowing that God exists, one then has to rely on faith alone and faith is separated from reason. When David Hume, who was really a latter-day Ockhamist, denied that we can know real causes, he stood in the tradition of mediæval English nominalists like Ockham.

Nominalists hold that general words like "virtue", "elasticity" and "power" do not name anything real in things but are applied by *convention* to many things or people. The examples of power and electricity are enough to render this doctrine doubtful. The nominalist only allows names to name individual things. There are just individual things which we call by the same name, for example "rose"; but we cannot see the relation between roses in nature or that they are all the same *kind* of thing. Thus we can only know what they are by intuition.

Nothing is universal in nature, according to nominalists, but only by its signification, as words, which are signs, are applied to many things: for example, the word "bear" to individual bears, which remain individual without sharing anything common in reality. A word is only common or universal by convention, not because there is anything common in nature. Only concepts are universal by nature for they are by definition general. But we cannot talk about individuals without talking about *kinds*, because to say that these two things are different is either to say that they are two individuals of the same kind or that they are two different kinds of thing.

However much nominalism may appeal to an instinctive tendency to doubt abstract concepts, we should also recognise its inadequate features.

ARGUMENTS AGAINST NOMINALISM

There are three main arguments against the nominalist position, which we will now examine in turn.

First, one could say that the word "peacock", for example, is just a name but is not the name of anything common or universal, which is shared by many things, because there is just this and that individual peacock in reality. Even granting this position, what reason would we have for calling anything a peacock unless peacocks *really* have a common nature? If they *really* have the same nature, this common nature also exists in reality, although it is only found in individual peacocks, and is not just an arbitrary invention of the human mind. How could anything that comes into existence be a peacock, unless the peacock nature already exists for new things to be able to share in and possess?

Second, some but not all words are just names. For example, "man" is used in two different ways, in "Socrates was a man" and "Man is a species". In the first, it is a predicate, meaning the human form or nature; in the second, it stands for a *kind*. The word "species" does not name an individual, as we may use the word "man" to refer to an individual with human nature: for example, "the man went to the well". "Man" may mean a kind and an individual, but nominalism does not allow for this distinction between the different ways we use the word, since it only recognises individuals in reality. According to nominalists, we are just talking about ideas when we say "Man is a species". Consider, for example, a sentence of good ordinary sense: "Man is mortal." What does "man" name here? Not a particular individual, nor a universal nature, but any and all human beings.

Third, nominalism does not allow us to speak of Christ in ways that are regarded as quite orthodox, because it does not recognise the different ways we may use the same word, sometimes as the name of an individual and sometimes as a predicate. For example:

a) God is man. "God" stands for an individual person with divine nature. "Man" here does not name an individual man but predicates human nature of a divine person, and says that this person also has human nature. Hence the subject and predicate have different roles: the subject stands for an individual, the predicate for a nature.

b) Christ is God. Here "God" does not name an individual, but predicates divine nature of the person who is called "Christ". "God" stands for divine nature.

c) Christ began to be man. In its orthodox sense, this does not mean that the person named "Christ" began to exist, for this person has always existed without beginning; rather it means that this person, who always existed with divine nature, began to exist in human nature as well. The eternal Son of God is called "Christ", because He became incarnate. If "man" names an individual here, as nominalists would have it, rather than predicated human nature of the subject, it would mean that Christ began to exist altogether.

d) God suffered. This does not predicate suffering of divine nature, since divine nature is immutable and impassible. God is not affected by things, otherwise some thing would be caused in him by other things, and the First Cause would no longer be the cause without a cause. This sentence predicates suffering of an individual person who is God, because he has divine nature, but *as* he also has human nature. God cannot suffer in his own nature but he can in human nature when this is united to divine nature in one person. We can say "God suffered" because the Son of God, who is the second Person of the Trinity, suffered in His human nature. Although we can say that God suffered, because the Son of God suffered, we cannot likewise say that the Father suffers, because the Father is not the Son, but a distinct Person, and human nature was not united to divine nature in the Father.

Unless we can use the words "God" and "man" in different ways, now standing for an individual person in the subject position, now for a nature in the predicate position, we end up by giving incorrect meanings to statements which have an orthodox sense. For instance, we would be asserting that the person named Christ, because he became man, had a beginning of existence, or that divine nature suffered. Names stand for the person, predicates for a nature; and predicates are not names, as the Two-Term Theory of the nominalists would make them.

Universal words are just signs for nominalists. The nominalist says, "I see two cats." They are different cats, because they are not one but two. But I cannot call them by the same name "cat" unless there is something that they both are. The question is whether this thing exists independently of them, as Plato thought; or is something real in things, as realists hold; or only exists in our minds, as nominalists hold. If two things are cats because they have a common nature, we face a dilemma.

This nature must be indivisible, or else it would only partly exist in each cat. But if it is indivisible, it must be one thing and cannot then exist in many. So it seems to exist on its own, independently of the many things we call cats. But if the cat nature cannot be shared by many, either there is only *one* real cat, which Plato called the Cat Idea, or there is nothing in reality whereby something else can be a cat, as nominalists hold. The nominalist cuts through the dilemma by denying that there are any such things as common natures in reality; so there is no problem for them about how the cat nature, for example, is shared by many, yet exists wholly in each cat.

Nominalists are compelled, however, to deny that the nature exists in what has the nature. In between the idealist and the nominalist comes the realist, who says that natures neither have real existence in another world of Ideas nor merely in our minds, but really exist in individuals in this world, for example in living peacocks, elephants, sheep and roses. Nominalists say that when we see two things which resemble one another, for example two bears or two cats, we form a concept and apply the word which is a sign of the concept to many individuals. But the realist asks: what is it in things which enables us to group many things under the same concept, for example "cat", if it does not exist in them but only in our minds?

For nominalists, only individuals exist in reality. For the realist, our general words also name something that exists in reality, though it is in individuals. The idealist disagrees with both, and either says that the real things are not the things in this world, but rather the Ideas, as Plato did, or that we cannot know real things in themselves, as Kant did. It is now time to give an outline of modern idealism, as we find it in the philosophy of Kant.

Chapter Ten

IDEALISM

Idealism is the philosophical outlook that starts from ideas rather than from things in this world. Its most important representative in modern times is Immanuel Kant (1724-1804). His idealism derives from Descartes, who made his starting-point the conscious mind. Descartes began by doubting the existence of the world around him, in order to arrive at knowing something that he could not doubt, namely the thought "I exist". Kant claimed to have introduced a "Copernican revolution" in thought, because he reversed the relation of thought and reality, just as Copernicus reversed our way of looking at the universe, so that it does not all go round us, but rather we around the sun. Kant's revolution was to say that the world is conformed to our ideas rather than our ideas to reality.

He held that the way we picture the world is conditioned by *a priori* ideas, rather than our ideas by the world. These ideas are the conditions of the way we know the world; Kant finds the conditions of our knowing in the mind rather than in the outside world. Knowledge for Kant is first grounded in the nature of our understanding, not in reality. Ideas do not derive from our experience of the world, but experience depends on the *a priori* ideas of our understanding; ideas are prior to our experience of the world, in Kant's view. He is an idealist, because he puts the mind before reality, but he is not an idealist like Plato, who thought that the Ideas exist outside us as independent objects; rather the source of ideas for Kant is our mind.

As Kant presents one of the main ways of looking at the world in modern times, but his system of thought is complex, it seems useful here to provide a simple explanation of his fundamental ideas, so that we can answer his criticisms of metaphysics.

A PRIORI IDEAS

We cannot think without thinking of something; there is no thought without content. The content first comes to us through the senses in perceiving things, but we cannot think of the content without *concepts*. Thus Kant says, "Thoughts without content are empty; intuitions without concepts are blind."[1] These concepts come from the understanding. Experience arises from the combination of sensation with ideas. For the British empiricists, Locke, Berkeley and Hume, experience *precedes* ideas; they are called empiricists, because they hold that all our ideas are derived *from* experience (*empeiria*). But Kant took the opposite view: as there is no experience without ideas, ideas precede experience and are therefore *a priori*.

---

[1] *Critique of Pure Reason* A51, B75.

Thus, ideas come from the mind rather than experience for Kant. Ideas come before experience for him, because they are what make experience possible at all. Experience arises when we arrange our sensations in certain patterns, which relate them and give them unity. Relation and unity are themselves two of Kant's categories of thought, which make experience possible. Thus, experience is more than mere sensation. As what arranges our sensations cannot itself be a sensation, it must be something else. Kant calls it an intuition (*Anschauung*). The understanding joins the manifold representations (*Vorstellungen*) which are given in *Anschauung* (intuition). The means by which we arrange what is given to intuition are the ideas, or categories, of thought. The categories are the ways that we *represent* objects to ourselves in experience. The categories will be described below.

ANALYTIC AND SYNTHETIC

There are two kinds of idea: *a priori* and *a posteriori*. *A priori* ideas can be known independently of experience of particular circumstances. They are *analytic* and necessary; they are analytic as they are contained in the very nature of the subject, and necessary as they follow from the definition of something: for example, a whole is greater than any of its parts. *A posteriori* ideas come from experience, because they are derived from it; they are synthetic, that is, we do not get them just by knowing something general, but have to know a little more about the particular circumstances of the object.

The difference between analytic and synthetic judgements comes out in the following example: "All bodies are extended" is an analytic judgement; if it is a body, it is extended, because all bodies take up space and have a measurement, however small it may be. But "These bodies are heavy" is a synthetic judgement; although all bodies have a weight, they are not necessarily heavy, for they may be light. Whether a body is heavy or light, we find out by experience of it.

All analytic statements are *a priori*, but Kant did not think that all synthetic statements are *a posteriori*. Mathematics may be thought to be *a priori*, because its truths are logical and necessary. For instance, to take Kant's example, 5 + 7 = 12 is necessary, because the correct result of this addition cannot be otherwise. But "5 + 7 = 12" is not an analytic statement, because five and seven are not necessarily contained in the idea of twelve; twelve may be four plus eight or nine plus three. Thus not all *a priori* judgements are analytic, and another sort of judgement in between is required for mathematics; this is the synthetic *a priori* judgement. Geometry, for example, may be *a priori* as it is a branch of mathematics, but it is not all analytic, for it depends on relations in space. So Kant's question became: how is it possible for us to make synthetic *a priori* judgements, which are required for mathematics?

Kant tells us that it was reading Hume and seeing that he did not allow for knowledge from synthetic *a priori* judgements, which awakened him from his "dogmatic slumbers". For Hume, and the empiricists, a statement was either analytic and *a priori* or synthetic and *a posteriori*, because derived from experience. They did not allow for any kind of judgement in between, that is *a priori* but synthetic. Kant thought that the derivation of all ideas from experience by the empiricist philosophers could not be reconciled with the nature of mathematics and physics, which contain truths we know *a priori*. According to the empiricists, it should not be possible to know truths of science *a priori*.

But some conceptions of science are *a priori* — for example, Newton's First Law, that a body keeps moving at the same speed in a straight line unless it is acted on by another force. We know this *a priori*, because no-one knows this from experience, as there always is another force acting on a body in the universe. Nonetheless, we know it to be true, because it can be deduced from the other laws of gravity. It has the form of a statement: if there were no other force acting on it, a moving body would continue at the same speed in a straight line. The movement of bodies that we observe is explained as the departure from continuing with a constant velocity in a straight line, because of other forces acting on them.

As not all statements of science are *a posteriori*, at least some of our ideas are *a priori*. The empiricists derived all conceptions from experience but did not make possible *a priori* conceptions in science. So to save this sort of knowledge in science, Kant derives conceptions from the understanding. Metaphysics for Kant is largely the question of how *a priori* synthetic judgements are possible, rather than knowledge of what *exists*.

KANT'S TWELVE CATEGORIES

Kant's theory is that we arrange our sensations with *a priori* conceptions of the understanding. These are his twelve categories of thought, which he divides into four sets of three.

1	Quantity	{Unity	(one)
		{Plurality	(many)
		{Totality	(whole)
2	Quality	{Reality	
		{Negation	
		{Limitation	

3	Relation	{Substance {Cause {Universal
4	Modality	{Possibility {Existence {Necessity

This list differs considerably from Aristotle's ten categories, which have served ordinary grammar for centuries. Where Aristotle's categories correspond with the ways in which things *exist*, Kant's correspond with the way the mind thinks and gives coherence to the phenomena we observe. Of Aristotle's categories, Kant only keeps substance and quantity, although he also finds room for place and time, but not as categories. Here it may suffice to give a brief account of two of Kant's categories: substance and cause, together with his ideas of space and time.

SUBSTANCE

How is this idea not derived from experience but presupposed by it, and so *a priori*? Kant notices that we have experience of things changing their appearances. How do I know that the appearances are of the same thing? For example, how do I know that the varying aspects of the moon from night to night are of the same object in the sky? All changes presuppose something *permanent* for Kant; this is the subject of change. We call the permanent thing underlying the changing appearances a substance. Everything we say about things is a determination of substance. We require the idea of substance, Kant says, to give unity to the successive phenomena we perceive, and so make what is given to the senses intelligible. We are affected by representations (*Vorstellungen*) of objects, but never know things in themselves. The way we get the idea of substance, for Kant, is not from external things but from our own consciousness.

The first way I come to the idea of substance, Kant says, is by reflecting that there is no experience without unity of consciousness, or apperception, as he calls it; but there can be no unity of consciousness unless *I* am a substance. So it is the awareness of myself that is the source of the idea of substance, which is therefore an *a priori* idea. Apperception is the self-conscious experience that this perception I am now having is mine.[2] The thought "I think" accompanies all my perceptions, Kant says, for I am immediately aware that *I* am perceiving and that this thought and perception are mine simultaneously. I do not perceive without thinking and knowing that I am perceiving. The unity of perception and thought does not derive from experience but is the very condition of having it. Thus the unity of apperception *precedes* experience, but there is no unity of apperception unless I am a substance: that is, the same permanent individual who has the successive perceptions. The idea of substance, then, is required as the condition, or possibility, of having experience. It is an *a priori* idea for Kant. We notice that Kant is more interested in the conditions of thought than in the existence of external things. For Aristotle, substance was the first of *existent* things.

CAUSE

Only by postulating permanent things, or substances, can we discover causes. Hume said that we could only know real causes if something could not be otherwise; in other words, if

---

[2] Ibid. A 107.

the connection between two things were necessary. But as we cannot know this, he said that cause is just an idea we get from the constant conjunction of two things: for example, the presence of copper in a fire and a blue flame. From Hume, Kant drew the conclusion that, as causes are necessary, the idea of cause is *a priori*. A cause is an idea of the mind for Kant, with which we explain our experience of successive phenomena and connect them. It is an *a priori* idea for Kant, because we do not deduce it from experience; instead, it is the condition of knowing the relation of phenomena. It is an idea rather than anything real.

For Kant, a cause means little more than the succession of phenomena; something is a cause if it comes before. A cause is a rule, by which phenomena precede and follow. It is a necessary connection, because all preceding states determine succeeding ones. If an effect does not necessarily follow, it is imaginary that it is connected.[3] He does not let us know the real causes, because we do not reach things in themselves, but remain on the level of appearances (*phenomena*). Nor does Kant allow us to apply the idea of cause to anything beyond experience, so that we could be led to know that God exists as the cause of the world.

SPACE AND TIME

Properly speaking, space and time are not categories of the understanding but *a priori* intuitions for Kant. They are *a priori*, because they are the conditions in which we experience all objects of the senses. Since they are *a priori*, we can think of space and time without anything in them; but we cannot think of things apart from space and time. Kant therefore thought

---

[3] Ibid. A 199/B 244.

that space and time are absolute; there is one space and one time, in which we perceive all things. We have no conception of motion without space, for motion is moving from one point to another; and no conception of change without time, for change is successive. Thus, space and time are *a priori* intuitions rather than conceptions, for we do not conceive of motion or change without them. As space and time are infinite, they do not belong to objects or things in themselves but come from the mind.

Time is that in which change occurs; time is not successive, but the phenomena are. Thus, it is absolute; there is only one time, in which everything happens. Time for Kant is a subjective condition of human intuition, the way we experience the succession of appearances. Thus, time is a way of representing objects to myself. Time is not anything in external things, because there would be no time but for our perceiving it. It is *a priori*, because we would not experience things as successive or simultaneous without first having the idea of time.[4]

It has to be said, however, that time is the measure of change, and there would be no time without change. Is time, then, the way we experience changing objects, or do we derive the idea of time from the experience of things changing? As there would be no time without change, it seems that time is not *a priori*, but that we get the idea of time from perceiving change, for it does not exist absolutely but only with things changing. We have to measure it by something, for instance the movement of the earth round the sun. Time is further considered in the Appendix.

---

[4] Ibid. A 32-34/ B 47-51.

PHENOMENA AND REALITY

Having established how we have subjective experience, Kant now has to show that an objective world exists. Since he derives our ideas from our understanding rather than from external things, how can we know that our ideas are not purely subjective? Kant gives two answers to this question. First, our knowledge is objective, because it is governed by universal laws of thought that are common to everyone. Secondly, the *a priori* ideas are objective, because I cannot conceive of myself as part of a world which disproves them.

Kant held that the categories of thought can only be applied to objects of which we can have experience. We may not, for example, apply the idea of cause to God, because God is not an object of experience. Nor can we apply the idea of cause to the world as a whole, because this goes beyond the bounds of sense. The only objects of experience for Kant are phenomena. We only know things as they affect us, not as they are in themselves; they affect us by representations (*Vorstellungen*). As the only objects of experience are phenomena, we can never know things in themselves or the *Dinge an sich*. A house is a phenomenon for Kant.[5] It follows that we cannot know the existence of anything which lies beyond the limits of experience.

We do not know substances, for instance, although we require the idea of substance to make intelligible our perception of changing phenomena as phenomena of the same object. Kant contrasts phenomena with *noumena*, a word he specially coins for things of which we have ideas but not experience. "Noumena" are objects of thought rather than experience. Kant includes God and the soul among noumena. The idea of God gives unity to the source of all existence, and

---

[5] Ibid. A 191/ B 236.

the soul unity to our experience and apperception. But we cannot know for certain that noumena exist. We come to them as explanations of our experience; we act as though they were true. But one may ask how we can explain the existence of anything, unless we can explain the existence of everything; that is, why there is anything at all.

As we only know phenomena, according to Kant, we cannot reach the real world behind the appearances. But how can we tell that appearances are appearances unless we also know the real world? Otherwise, they may be the real things, for all that we know. To call something an appearance, implies that it is the appearance of something. It is not possible to know that anything is a phenomenon unless we also know real things. These criticisms of Kant also apply to the view of phenomenalism: that things just consist of sense-data, because all we directly know of things is our sense impressions of them. The phenomenalist is not justified in calling anything a phenomenon unless we also know real things, with which to compare it. How do we know there is a real world if we only know phenomena? But also, how do we know that things are just phenomena unless we also know reality?

Kant calls his philosophy "transcendental", because it is about the conditions of knowing anything and the categories of thought are deduced from the mind. It is also transcendental because my "I" is not part of the world but outside it, just as the eye is not part of the visual field but remains outside it. For Kant, the only reality which is immediately clear to me is myself; the rest may be only phenomena. Kant thought that I am conscious of myself independently of the world, just by thinking; but he forgot that we are first conscious of ourselves as distinct from the world around us, because we have a body.[6] It seems odd to do "transcendental" philosophy and deny that we can know the existence of anything transcendent, that is, beyond the limits of sense-experience. How do I know that these are the limits of nature unless I can transcend them? Otherwise, I do not know that there is nothing beyond my horizon.

The philosophy of Kant presents us with an understanding of our understanding rather than of reality; it stays within the realm of thought. If it seems more like epistemology than metaphysics, nonetheless it has been necessary to examine it, since Kant's claim that we cannot go beyond the limits of sense in applying our categories of thought has provided what many in modern times have considered to be a powerful argument against the very possibility of metaphysics. We do not know our knowing, however, unless we first know something, for it is by having thoughts and perceptions that we know our minds. But we do not know anything unless it is real. Thus, we may oppose to the idealism of Kant our third main view of the world, which is realism.

---

[6] Ibid. B 417.

Chapter Eleven

REALISM

When talking about realism, we should first make clear what we mean by a realist, for two quite different philosophical outlooks are called "realist". It has been common to call Plato a realist, because he made his Ideas the real things, of which things in this world are copies and images. As he makes ideas the primary things, he may also be regarded as an idealist. But he is not an idealist like Kant: Plato's Ideas exist as independent objects, whereas ideas for Kant come from the human mind. The great difference between Plato and modern idealists is that Plato looks *outwards* at an objective, although invisible and immaterial, world of the Ideas existing outside our minds, but Kant looks *inwards* at the ideas of his own mind. Plato is objective, where modern idealists are subjective about ideas, because they start from the consciousness of themselves. This subjective turn in philosophy at the beginning of the modern era was brought about by Descartes (1596-1650), who made his own conscious mind the starting-point of his philosophy. In this respect, the idealism of Kant derives from Descartes.

I take realism to be the doctrine that, first, there is an external world, and, second, it is possible for us to know the real world. The realist is objective and starts with the thought that "this exists"; the modern idealist is subjective and begins by saying, "I am." Idealists confuse the way things exist with the way we think of them: either like Plato, who thought that the real things exist like ideas, which is immaterially; or like Kant, who said that the world is conformed to our ideas rather than our ideas to the world.

Just as Plato held that the Ideas are the real things, nominalists say that the only real things are individuals, not the universal Ideas of things. Aquinas, however, held that universals only exist in the mind, as they only exist when they are thought of. Natures are individual in their real existence, and only general in our thought. The swan nature, for example, only has real existence in individual swans, which are the real swans. Plato held that the Swan Idea, which was the Swan itself, the essence of a swan, existed independently of being thought of by anyone; but Aquinas held that universal ideas only exist in minds through being thought of. Nonetheless, Aquinas also thought that universal ideas are of something that exists in reality. Nominalists, on the other hand, held that universal ideas are merely ideas; our universal words are merely names (*nomina*), which name nothing existing in reality.

Aristotle remarks that, if the only things which exist in reality are individuals, we have no objects of thought, for knowledge is by its nature *universal*.[1] For example, I do not just perceive individual flowers but can know *what* they are; to

---

[1] *Metaphysics* B (III) c.6 1003a14.

recognise anything as a violet is straightaway to know that it has something in common with other individual flowers, which we also identify as violets. The reason why I think that bricks, for instance, are red is because they have something in common with other things that are also red. Thus we have the universal idea of red, which applies to all red things. The nominalist thinks that we invent these ideas; the realist, that we discover what resides in nature herself.

The differences between these three fundamental ways of looking at the world, idealist, realist and nominalist, may be made plain in the diagram below.

	Universal ideas	Philosopher
Idealist	The real things	Plato
Realist	Ideas of the mind, but of something existing in reality	Aquinas
Nominalist	Merely ideas of the human mind, but of nothing in reality	Locke

To these three fundamental outlooks, we may add a fourth: phenomenalism, which is widespread in English philosophy today, as it derives from the empiricist philosophers, Locke, Berkeley and Hume. For it follows from their philosophy that, if what I immediately know is not things themselves, but the impressions they make on my senses (that is, sense-data), things may just consist of sense-data. Physical things are as much a myth for phenomenalists as universal ideas are for nominalists; there are just impressions in the senses. The phenomenalist only sees the appearances of a penny, while the realist sees a penny itself. The realist knows that it is round, even though its appearance may be elliptical when seen at a certain angle.

Two points may be made against the phenomenalist. First, if all that I know is appearances or sense-data, how do I know that they are of external things? For if all that I know is appearances, they may be the only things, and I may live in a world of illusions without any reality behind it. Second, I do not look at the impressions external objects make in my eye, as I look at the things outside me. I cannot look at images on my retina as I can at a tree; images are not what I look at but that *by which* I see something, such as a tree.[2] But what I look at is the tree itself; the image it makes in my eye is that *by which* I see it. We should not confuse the impression with the reality, or the thing we see with the means by which we perceive it with the senses.

THE REAL WORLD

We have two questions. First, are individuals the only things that exist in reality, or are natures also real? And second, do we only know ideas or can we also know real things?

In answer to the first of these questions, if ducks have the nature of ducks, where does this duck nature exist? Plato says that the duck nature exists on its own as the Duck Idea, and that this is the real duck. The nominalist says that the general idea of a duck is nothing in reality; there are just individual things in reality, which we call ducks, although they do not *really* have anything in common. The realist says that the idea is of something real in nature.

Against Plato, the realist says that universal ideas exist in the mind rather than in reality; against the nominalist, he says that universal ideas are not just inventions of the mind, but of something in reality. Essences neither exist on their own, as Plato held, nor are they just inventions of the mind, as

---

[2] Aquinas, *Summa theologiae* I q.85, 2. This article of Aquinas is enough to refute Locke, who makes ideas the things we know.

nominalists hold, but are really found in individuals. The idealist cuts out real things — either, like Plato, by saying that things in this world are not the real ones or, like Kant, by saying that we cannot know real things in themselves. The nominalist cuts out real natures. The realist, however, keeps *both*: real things in this world and real natures. To both questions, the realist replies that natures exist in reality *and* that we can know real things. Thus the realist holds a middle position between idealism and nominalism. Essences do not exist on their own, as Plato thought, but only in individuals; but natures *are* real and not just ideas, as nominalists regard them. The real things that we know are individuals, not universal ideas, as Plato held; but our universal ideas are of something that exists in nature and of the world as it really is, not just the way we see it.

In this, the realist differs from an idealist like Kant, who says that the way we think the world is constructed is conditioned by certain ideas which we have *a priori*, such as space, time, relation, unity and his other categories. These ideas are *a priori* for Kant, because we possess them *before* experience; they are what enable us to have experience by making intelligible the phenomena we observe in sensation. Thus, our view of the world is determined by the mind's ideas. The question is, whether the way we think the world is depends on our ideas, or whether our ideas depend on the way the world really is. For the idealist, the world depends on our ideas; for the realist, the world exists independently of our thought and language. For Kant, our ideas are the measure of reality; for the realist, reality is the measure of my thought. My thought is true when it matches reality. We shall return to this point in a moment, when we come to truth. But first, what reason have we for thinking that there is an external world whose existence does not depend on our minds, but is independent of us? In other words, can I know the real world and real things in themselves, which is the second of the two questions we posed above?

Etienne Gilson gives the following reasons for saying that we can know the real world. First, the existence of the world is not just a postulate we make to explain the phenomena, as physicists postulate new particles (quarks, anti-protons etc.) to explain effects they have observed, although they have not yet proved the existence of these latest kinds of particle. We know the world through our senses; its existence is *evident* to us from the testimony of the senses. The testimony of the senses is, on the whole, reliable; otherwise, if the senses were often mistaken, we would be unable to tell the difference between illusion and reality and have to resign ourselves to scepticism, unable to know what is true and false.

The realist holds that we know there is a real world outside us, because we *perceive* it with the senses. Ideas and thought are not the only principles of knowledge; the senses, too, know things. It is often forgotten that sensation is a way of *knowing* things. Ideas are the starting-point of knowledge for idealists, but sense-impressions are so for a realist like Aquinas. But Aquinas does not remain simply an empiricist, because he thinks that we can go *beyond* what the senses tell us, in forming general concepts from our sense-impressions. As Aquinas says, "our knowledge (*cognitio*) has its beginning in sensation"; but it is only the beginning. What the senses tell us is not the end.

Kant, however, does not allow us to go beyond the phenomena or to apply our categories of thought (cause, existence etc.) to anything beyond what we know from the senses. In Kant's view, we construct the world according to our ideas, which we may only apply to the phenomena of this world. It is the same with the empiricist Hume, who makes ideas just be faded impressions, so that we cannot go beyond what we know by the experience of the senses. The difference between Kant and an empiricist like Hume is that, for Kant, we need ideas to turn sensation into experience, whereas for empiricists, sensation already is experience by itself. But as the empiricists hold that the immediate objects of our knowledge are ideas or perceptions, they do not allow us to know that there is a real world outside us.

One thing that we know, however, is that our knowledge is *caused*, otherwise we would be the makers of the things we knew. Either *we* cause our knowledge, or it is caused by *real* things outside our minds. The world does not impress itself on us in any way; we do not just see the world in a certain way but the *world* affects the way we see. If I cannot know the real world but all that I know is ideas and perceptions, as Locke and Hume held, how do I know that my ideas are caused by external reality? For all I know, they may come from my mind. If, on the other hand, the idealism of Kant is true, there seems to be no reason why scientists all over the world agree about the way it is and do not construct different worlds from their ideas. As they agree, for otherwise there would not be one natural science throughout the world, our thought is conditioned by the world, not the world by our thought.

For Kant, the world is a product of the understanding's categories of thought; for the realist, thought reflects the structure of the world and language is founded on the way things are in nature. For Hume, on the other hand, the external world is a product of the imagination, working on impressions. Hume more or less confines the mind to the imagination, because ideas are faded impressions and so are mental images rather than concepts. All that we have, according to Hume, is experience, which is the sum of our impressions and mental images. Although Hume did not explicitly deny the existence of the real world, he said that we have no *reason* to believe that it exists; we just *infer* its existence from our perceptions. John Searle, however, rightly points out that it does not follow that, because "Experience is the basis of all knowledge", all we know is what we experience.[3] There is an external world, because experience is not the object of my perception; perceiving some object is the experience. If experiences are what I perceive, we would not even have any perceptions, for perceptions first require outside objects.

REALISM AND TRUTH

But what does it mean to say that our thoughts reflect the structure of the world? We may express it like this.[4] First, we distinguish between knowing individuals and knowing things generally. Things have individual existence; I *think* of them generally. Let us take as our example a horse called "Bronco". Bronco is an individual instance of the horse nature; the horse nature has actual existence in Bronco. The horse nature also has *natural* existence in Bronco. When I think of Bronco, a horse has *intentional* existence in my mind.[5] The same form that exists naturally in Bronco exists intentionally in my mind when I think of a horse. Its existence in my mind is called "intentional", because it is the object of my thought. When I think of a horse, there is the same form in my mind as in a horse. My concept of a horse is a likeness of the horse's nature. It is having the same form which makes things like one

---

[3] *The Social Construction of Reality* (Allen Lane, 1995), p. 171.

[4] J. Haldane, C.Wright (edd.), *Reality, Representation and Projection* (Oxford, 1993), pp. 21f.

[5] See Aquinas, *Summa theologiae* I q. 56, 2 ad 3 for natural and intentional existence.

another. The same form exists in two ways: naturally in a horse and intentionally in the mind with the thought of a horse. The mind is then *informed* with the form of a horse when it thinks of a horse. Thus, the mind is *conformed* with the formal structure of reality, for the same form is in my mind as in the real thing. The truth of my thought consists in the *correspondence* of the content of my mind with reality.

Thus, realism goes with the correspondence theory of truth. This theory of truth says that our thought is true when there is a matching (*adaequatio*) of the mind with the thing or reality.[6] "Real" comes from the Latin word for thing, *res*. The mind is conformed with the formal structure of reality when it has the same form as there is in nature: for example, the horse form in thinking of a horse. When I think of a horse, there is, so to speak, a horse in my mind. But the matter of a horse is not in my mind; so its *form* is.

The correspondence theory of truth, however, is widely questioned today. John Searle, for example, has recently called for a return to realism at the same time as discarding the correspondence theory of truth. Realism for Searle means that the world exists independently of my representations of it. It does not mean that we know *how* things exist but only *that* there is a way they are, which is logically independent of the mind.

Searle points out that the understanding of many sentences presupposes external reality, for example, "Mont Blanc is covered with snow", even when they are false. For Searle, it is enough that sentences claim to refer to phenomena that are accessible to others. The question is whether there *are* any phenomena, and whether we are right in assuming that there is an external reality. Searle seeks to take the very thing

---

[6] *Summa theologiae* I q.16, 2.

that is under discussion for granted.[7] Our statements only show that there is the external reality, which Searle says they presuppose *if they are true.* At some point, we have to make a *judgment* by comparing what we say or think with things or objects, that is, with external, objective reality. Unless we can know the real world itself, and not just that there is a real world, how do we know that the world our statements presuppose is not constructed from language and the way we happen to speak? On Searle's view, the world may be constructed from language, just as it is by ideas in Kant. Reality is not constructed by society, but our ability to understand one another rests on our knowing a reality that is independent of human minds. We do not know that our sentences presuppose external reality unless we can know this reality itself.

The end of the mind is to know the truth. The end of metaphysics is, likewise, to come to the truth, because it is about what exists. Truth is founded on the *existence* of things, for we have said that our minds are not the measure of reality, but that reality is the measure of truth in our minds. The last end of metaphysics is to come to the first Truth, which is the source of all existence, as the universe comes from a Mind. But as philosophy is also meant to be *wisdom*, metaphysics has practical consequences for how we act well. We shall note some of these consequences in seeing how metaphysics provides a foundation for ethics.

---

[7] *The Social Construction of Reality*, pp. 185-189.

Chapter Twelve

METAPHYSICS AND ETHICS

Human beings are set above all other visible things by their understanding. The sun and stars, for instance, do not know how they work. We know how things are connected and how one thing will produce another. Our knowledge of causes enables us to choose the means which will lead to the ends we conceive. Thus we base our actions on what we know. The realist knows four things: first, he knows *real* things; second, that they have definite *natures*; third, that they have a purpose or *end*; fourth, that all these things constitute a cosmos, that is, an *ordered* whole.[1] Let us examine these four points in turn.

First, then, we know how things really are, not just as they affect us or with the pattern we impose on things; rather we discern the pattern in things.

Second, from this it follows that we know that things have definite natures, because these natures are not just our arbitrary division of things, or inventions of our mind, but

---

[1] I owe these four points to a letter from Mr. Philip Trower.

have real existence in things. As things have natures, it follows that there is a way they are normally meant to be. Ostriches are meant to have long necks. If an ostrich were born with a short neck, this would be abnormal; it would be deformed. Everything has its proper form and way of acting; in other words, there is a way it *ought* to be. Chemists construct experiments by assuming that chemicals ought to act in certain ways with other chemicals in certain conditions. As things have a right form, so they have a right way of acting. A wrong action is like a deformed action; it does not correspond with the thing's proper form or nature. Its right way of acting comes from its nature.

Third, as things have a right way of acting, which is in conformity with their nature, so they have a purpose and end. They are meant to achieve their end. The end of a plant, for example, is to reach its full growth, to flower and so to reproduce itself. If the highest power of human nature, our understanding, does not arise from matter by itself, then our end lies *beyond* the material universe in something higher than it. We can see that things have an end: eyes are meant to see, acorns to produce new oak trees. Whatever is contrary to something achieving its end, which is to exist and act according to its nature, is bad for it. Likewise, actions that are contrary to, or obstruct, our purpose and end are bad.

Fourth, the idea of an end involves being *ordered* to an end. We see that there is order in the universe: the heavenly bodies keep their place, so that there is not chaos. The very idea of trying to conserve nature implies that everything has its right place, which we ought not to disregard. There is order in the universe as a whole, because not only are things ordered to their own ends, but they are all ordered *to one another*. Like the different instruments of an orchestra, they have a unity, as we see from the order of the universe. Things would not be ordered to one another, and not just to their own individual end, unless they had been given their order and end by *one* mind. Their unity comes from one source. Order comes from a mind, because it neither comes from chance nor from matter alone, which cannot conceive the end for which it acts. The order of the universe comes from one mind, because if it were from more than one, there would be conflict, and so chaos rather than order in the universe. Things can only be directed to the same end by one mind determining their end.

As the universe displays an overall order, only something *outside* the universe can have given it its order; nothing within the universe, or any part of it, could have given it its order as a whole. As the order of the universe comes from outside itself, the end of the universe, which is the *final* end of everything, lies beyond the universe. This is one reason why we need metaphysics, because physics or natural science does not take us beyond the material universe, although we can tell from it that the order of the universe has an external origin.

We go beyond the visible universe, because matter does not order itself. We notice that lumps of matter very often have no definite shape or order but are piled in a heap, like stones and rocks by the side of a river. Matter is given form and order by intelligent beings. The order of the universe is itself a model of society: as the good of nature is that everything is ordered to the whole, so our actions are good when they preserve the good of the whole, which is also the good of the individuals in it. Nothing that damages the good of a part can be for the good of the whole, as we know from the human body. This rules out utilitarian ethics, which looks to the supposed good and happiness of the greatest number but without insisting that an action also has to be right for the doer. What comes from the bad will of any one member cannot be for the good of the society as a whole, since damage to one part of the body affects the whole body. Also every individual has an end beyond society in this life; so unless his or her action is also in conformity with this higher end, it will also be to the detriment of society as it means that the doer's will is not directed rightly to the individual's proper end.

If things in nature have ends, as we see that they do, it is because they have been given their ends by someone who thought of their ends. Moreover, things only have an order because they are directed to an end. The parts of a plant or an animal clearly are directed to an end: that it lives, preserves itself and functions with its complete powers. The things we make, like machines and tools, get their end from their maker or inventor. Likewise, the universe has order, because it has been given its end by its Maker. Once you do away with a maker, there is no way things are meant to be or to act, and you cannot tell how things ought to be, because they do not have a purpose or end. Purpose comes from being designed to do something, as wings are designed for flying, whether they be the wings of birds or aeroplanes. Without a maker, things do not have an end, because no one has designed them. And without an end, there is no way that they are meant to act. Thus ethics, which is about right and wrong ways for us to act, is connected with metaphysics, inasmuch as metaphysics leads us to see that the world does not explain itself but has a cause beyond itself, and that each thing in it is as it is, because its nature was conceived by the mind who made it.

The consequences for ethics of doing away with the Maker can be seen in the philosophies of Hume and Kant.[2] Empiricists and idealists deprive themselves of contact with reality, which is the foundation of ethics. For Hume, all that

---

[2] As Philip Trower pointed out to me in the same letter.

we directly know is our perceptions, rather than the things which cause impressions in us. We do not know real things in themselves, but only *infer* that they exist as the causes of our perceptions. Kant likewise says that all we know is phenomena, not things in themselves. Thus we just have a stream of impressions with Hume, or of ideas with Kant; but neither of them allows us to have contact with reality.

As the world is either a product of our imagination for Hume, or a construction of our mind from its *a priori* ideas for Kant, nothing has an end. Consequently, there is no way things *ought* to act, because the world comes from *our* minds, rather than from a Mind which has given everything its proper nature and end. As Hume denies that we can find out the real causes of things, we cannot explain order in the universe or, therefore, discern purpose, which involves things being ordered to an end. Kant, however, finds a place for order, but says that it is imposed on the phenomena by our minds. Thus, Kant abandons the means of recognising how things ought to be in nature, but as he wants to preserve the moral law, he has to make it an inner command of our minds rather than the command of a mind which has established the right way for everything to act in accordance with its nature.

The realist, however, unlike the empiricist Hume and the idealist Kant, can see that things have been given their proper natures by a mind that has ordered everything in the universe. Thus virtuous action, which is right action, corresponds with our rational nature and is directed to our proper end. But our end lies beyond the visible world of nature, for the power of reason and understanding does not arise from matter below, since it reflects *on* it from above. No other corporeal beings that we know of, besides us, reflect on themselves or on the world around them. If any other beings do so, they too like ourselves are above the purely material. As we are raised above matter by our ability to reflect on it, we have an end which is higher than the physical universe.

Metaphysics provides the foundation for ethics, because it shows us that something *exists* beyond the things studied by physics, to which we can direct our lives. We cannot direct our lives to something higher than this world unless we know that it exists. But once we recognise that there is something higher than this world, this will determine the way we think we ought to direct our lives. As the highest power of human nature is the intellect, and the intellect is for seeing the truth, so our final end is to come to see the First Truth.

APPENDIX

TIME

One might hold that the topic of time belongs to physics rather then metaphysics, because it has to do with measurement and motion. Yet time raises questions which natural science does not answer by itself. I shall confine myself here to two main questions about time: first, is time real, and second, is it a fourth dimension, or are space and time quite different ways of perceiving things?

THE REALITY OF TIME

Time is the succession of one thing after another. There is no time without change. The Cambridge philosopher McTaggart (1866-1925) argued that time is unreal, because change does not occur. He thought that there is no change in reality when, if one thing changes, everything else also changes. When one thing moves, something else is moved, and so there is a series of reactions throughout the universe by the "knock-on" effect. This is true of what are called "Cambridge changes". A Cambridge change occurs when something changes in relation to other things because something else changes, although it does not change in itself. A standard example of this is when Socrates is first taller, then shorter than Theætetus, because Theætetus grows taller. There is only a Cambridge change of Socrates, for he remains the same height, but a *real* change of Theætetus. When I face southwards, supposing that I stand in the northern hemisphere, the sun changes its position relative to me, from being on my left in the early morning to my right side in the afternoon. This is not a real change of the sun but of the earth in its movement round the sun. Peter Geach points out that no Cambridge changes occur without something *actually* changing. Therefore, Cambridge changes are not the only kind of change, and some changes are real. With change comes time.[1]

McTaggart also argued that time is unreal, because events do not change. The battle of Waterloo, for example, is not a different event now from what it was when it was being fought in 1815. An event does not have a history or change with time. Two points can be made against this view. First, events come about by the change of existing things, as we saw in Chapter Five on existence. Secondly, when the battle of Waterloo was over, the event no longer existed in the same way as when it was being fought; it was then *past*.

Events occur one after another in succession; and with the succession of things there is time. Even when there is no means of measuring time, for instance on a planet that is covered with cloud, it still makes sense to talk of now and then, before and after, and together (at the same time) of one thing in relation to another. There would still be past, present and future, even when time could not be measured. It is this very difference of things between having passed, being present or still to come that requires us to speak of time.

If there is no time, everything is simultaneous. The view that time is unreal implies that we can see everything as God sees it, if there is only the present. There is no time for God, because everything is present to Him, as He is outside the world, for He encompasses the universe He has made. But we do not have this sort of view of the universe: things have

---

[1] P.T. Geach, *Truth, Love and Immortality* (Hutchinson, 1979), pp. 89-103.

passed out of our sight and other things that still lie ahead have not yet come into our view.

Geach argues against McTaggart that, if it is an illusion that states of things are past, present and future, at least the illusions are not simultaneous, for we know that one illusion comes after another. So our illusions are not all simultaneous but occur in succession, and there is time after all. The idea of some things being earlier and others later gives the idea of time. "Earlier" does not just mean "past", nor "later" simply "future", for we can talk about "earlier than" and "later than" of past events, and also of one thing being earlier than another in the future. For St. Augustine, the past is time that has gone away, the future time that has not yet arrived; only the present is existent time.

Does this mean that there is no time, because the past and future are not real and there is only the present? We may distinguish between time and times. No one time ever occurs twice: 5.29 p.m. on 27th July, 1973, only occurred once. This point of time no longer exists, for it has passed. Times are like points marked on a measuring rod that is moved at an even speed across the same point. When it passes this point, it is the time that is marked on the measuring rod. There are no times without time.

To say that time is unreal is like saying that one word does not come after another on the printed page, because we can see all the words on one page simultaneously. Although we can see all the words at a glance, we cannot read or utter them all at once but only one at a time in succession.

SPACE-TIME

Time used to be regarded as different from space; now it is usually regarded as a fourth dimension of objects which are conceived as extended in time as well as in space.[2] It is possible to view objects in this way when time and length are made the two axes on which an object is represented. From this point of view, time is a dimension in which bodies are extended. Thus, a poker, for example, which has different temperatures at different times is like one long poker with different temperatures at different points along it as it is extended through time. One could talk about St. Paul's Cathedral in 1801 and St. Paul's Cathedral in 1856 as two sections of St. Paul's in the nineteenth century. This would make St. Paul's in 1801 and St. Paul's in 1856 into *parts* of St. Paul's seen in its entire extension through time. Yet St. Paul's did not partly exist in 1801 and partly in 1856, but wholly at either time; it was as much present in 1801 as in 1856.

As Geach points out, "St. Paul's in 1801" is not a logical subject; rather, St. Paul's alone is the subject, whether it is in 1801 or in 1856. If time is a fourth dimension in which objects are extended, they never wholly exist at any one time, but are only parts of objects that are only complete when all the times in which they exist are taken together. When time is seen as a fourth dimension, St. Paul's in 1801 has to be different from St. Paul's in 1856, because they are different sections and parts of the cathedral extended through the nineteenth century. However, we can say that the same object existed in 1856 as in 1801; they were not two different parts. McTaggart in 1879 and 1911 are not two slices of one philosopher who is only whole when his existence is complete. If "me at 1950" and "me at 1990" are two bits of me, I would never be whole at any point of my duration in time. To our ordinary way of thinking, a mercury thermometer has only one temperature at

---

[2] For a criticism of the view of time as a fourth dimension, see P.T. Geach, "Some Problems about Time", in *Logic Matters* (Blackwell, 1972), pp.302-318.

a time. With time as a fourth dimension of it, a thermometer would have many temperatures along its extension through time. This view of time contradicts Heraclitus' saying that you cannot step into the same river twice, for it *would* be possible to step into the same river twice, if different times are just different points along its entire length.

The view that time is a fourth dimension of objects abolishes changes by saying that the variation of its states are different parts of one whole, rather than changes of one whole thing. This view dispenses with change as unreal but keeps time. Yet there is no time without change. It also confuses states of the same object with parts of it. An object can remain whole, although its states change. As Roderick Chisholm remarks, temporal parts of the history of a substance are not parts, but *states* of the individual. Temporal slices of a thing's history are not also slices of the thing that has the history.[3]

Time and space are two quite different categories. Space is *here* and time is *now*. Space has to do with above and below and at the side of; time with before and after. We measure space and time in different ways. To measure space, we measure the object itself; to measure time, we measure one object against something independent, such as a clock, or by the movement of the earth round the sun. Space has to do with size and magnitude, time with motion and existence. Size inheres in the object itself; an object can remain the same size but not always exist in the same time.

Time is the measurement of motion. We measure time by distance and distance by time. In this respect, time may be counted as a dimension of space. Time is measured by space: twenty-four hours is the interval between the crossing of a meridian twice by the same star. And we measure space by

---

[3] *A Realistic Theory of Categories* (Cambridge, 1996), pp. 93 and 76.

time: a metre is the distance travelled by particles of krypton, shot in a tube, in a certain time. The measurement of space and time cannot be separated. A poster advertising the museum of the Royal Observatory at Greenwich describes it as "the centre of space and time". This seems to contradict the view that all time is relative, for then no one point would have any advantage over another. But time is taken from a mean time, which is at Greenwich, and this is the time at a certain point in space. If all times are to agree, as they can if we are talking about the existence of the same universe, they must be taken from reference to one time. Space is distance traversed by light in a certain time, roughly 300,000 kilometres in one second. When we measure time by distance, we assume that the velocity of light is *constant*.

The speed of light provides an objective standard of measuring motion. This means that not all time is merely relative, according to the movement of an observer relative to other bodies in the universe. Time is relative in the sense that we can only measure it by the movement of one body against another. But it is not relative in the sense that the same event occurs at different times for different observers. If two observers are moving in opposite directions, two events that are simultaneous for one of the observers will not be so for the other, who will perceive one sooner or later than the other as he is moving towards or away from it, because light takes time to travel. The only signal we receive of an event is by the light that travels from an object.

Because of this, an observer who is moving away from the point of an event at a great speed may perceive something that came before as coming after. According to this view, something might be a cause or an effect, if it can be seen as either before or after by different observers. But of two events, only one can be the cause of the other, for a cause must exist before an effect. If something really is the cause, it cannot come after, however it may be perceived by an observer. The Second Law of Thermodynamics indicates that time proceeds in one direction, for some processes cannot be reversed. One cannot reverse the flow of a river, so that water leaves its spring after it flows into the sea. The past cannot be in the future. With things coming one after another in an unchangeable order, we have time; the same thing cannot be either past or future. Although there is no time but for perceivers of the things that move, time is not entirely subjective but real.

INDEX